The publisher of this book is generously donating all royalties from the retail sales of **"STRESS-FREE DIVORCE: VOLUME 02"** to:

LEMONADE DAY

America was built on the back of small business. Entrepreneurs take risks believing they can realize their dream if they work hard, take responsibility and act as good stewards of their resources. Today's youth share that optimism, but lack the life skills, mentorship and real-world experience necessary to be successful. In 2007, founder Michael Holthouse had a vision to empower today's youth to become tomorrow's entrepreneurs through helping them start, own and operate their very own business...a lemonade stand.

Lemonade Day is a strategic 14-step process that walks youth from a dream to a business plan, while teaching them the same principles required to start any big company. Inspiring kids to work hard and make a profit, they are also taught to spend some, save some and share some by giving back to their community. Since its launch in 2007 in Houston Texas, Lemonade Day has grown from serving 2,700 kids in one city to 1 million children across North America. With the help of partners like Google for Entrepreneurs, Lemonade Day will continue to spark the spirit of entrepreneurship and empower youth to set goals, work hard, and achieve their dreams.

You can learn more about
Lemonade Day by visiting: www.LemonadeDay.org

STRESS-FREE DIVORCE
VOLUME 02

Conversations With
Leading Divorce Professionals

By Remarkable Press™

Stress-Free Divorce: Volume 02/ Mark Imperial. —1st ed.

Managing Editor/ Stewart Andrew Alexander

ISBN: 978-0998708539

CONTENTS

A NOTE TO THE READER

Thank you for buying your copy of "Stress-Free Divorce Volume 02: Conversations With Leading Divorce Professionals." This book was originally created as a series of live interviews, that's why it reads like a series of conversations, rather than a traditional book that talks at you.

I wanted you to feel as though the participants and I are talking with you, much like a close friend, or relative, and felt that creating the material this way would make it easier for you to grasp the topics and put them to use quickly, rather than wading through hundreds of pages.

So relax, grab a pen and paper, take notes and get ready to learn some fascinating, stress-free divorce insights.

Warmest regards,

Mark Imperial
Author and Radio Personality

INTRODUCTION

"Stress-Free Divorce Volume 02: Conversations With Leading Divorce Professionals" is a collaborative book series featuring leading Divorce Professionals from across the country.

Remarkable Press™ would like to extend a heartfelt thank you to all participants who took the time to submit their chapter and offer their support in becoming 'get the word out ambassadors' for this project.

100% of the royalties from the retail sales of this book will be donated to Lemonade Day. Should you want to make a direct donation, visit their website at:

www.LemonadeDay.org

NANCY A. HETRICK, CDFA®, MAFF®

Divorce Financial Planner, and Mediator

Smarter Divorce Solutions, LLC

Email: Nancy@SmarterDivorceSolutions.com

Website: www.SmarterDivorceSolutions.com

LinkedIn: www.linkedin.com/in/nancyhetrick

Twitter: www.twitter.com/NancyAHetrick

Call: (877) 552-4017

Nancy founded Smarter Divorce Solutions in 2011 after going through her own less-than-optimal divorce. She has over 18 years of experience in investment management and financial planning as a financial advisor with Better Money Decisions in addition to the divorce services she provides as a Certified Divorce Financial Analyst at Smarter Divorce Solutions.

In 2016, Nancy founded the Divorce Financial Planner Training Center (http://divorcefinancialtraining.com) to offer continuing education and professional development to CDFA® holders everywhere.

Nancy is a Master Analyst in Financial Forensics, (MAFF™), a Certified Divorce Financial Analyst (CDFA®), an Accredited Wealth Management Advisor (AWMA), an Accredited Asset Management Specialist (AAMS), a Chartered Mutual Fund Counselor (CMFC) and a trained mediator.

Nancy is on the board of the Collaborative Professionals of Phoenix and the Arizona Association for Conflict Resolution and was the Finance Director for the National Association of Women Business Owners, 2014 and 2015, the 2015 NAWBO Business Owner of the Year, the 2014 Finalist in the BBB Business Ethics Awards, was on the 2014 National Board of Advisors for the Institute for Divorce Financial Analysts, and is a frequent volunteer for the Fresh Start Foundation for Women.

THE TOP 6 STUPID MISTAKES
MADE IN DIVORCE SETTLEMENTS
By Nancy A. Hetrick

I feel strongly that not enough people in the world of divorce professionals will truly tell it like it is, even if it's not what you want to hear. I make it a regular practice to share with my clients the full and complete truth so that that no matter what choices they make, they make them fully informed. So here it comes. Let me help you NOT be stupid!

I see a few things over and over again when it comes to divorce settlements that were agreed to, and sometimes even ordered by a judge, where the people come to me after-the-fact confused and bewildered and I read through their decree and just shake my head. Please, please, please – DON'T make these mistakes!

#6 – Making Emotional Decisions Instead of Financial

There are two emotional states that are very common for divorcing parties that can get you into trouble. The first is being too passive and the second is being too aggressive.

There's a very real psychological phenomenon that happens when you are in the midst of divorce. The emotions of the situation require a tremendous amount of energy and for each unit of energy being consumed by extreme emotions is one less unit of energy that is available for logical, rational thinking. I have often heard my clients describe themselves as having "brain fog" and many blogger have written about "divorce brain". You hear information but struggle to process it or place things into long-term context with a clear picture of consequences. During this time, it is critical that you have an advocate to ensure that the details are all being addressed to protect yourself.

The burden of extreme emotions can manifest in a passive way when people going through divorce just want to "get it over with" and will agree to settlements just to be done. This kind of thinking in divorce can lead to bankruptcy. A hopeless, passive approach leads people to give up far more than they should, accept less support than they are entitled to, or give in to pressure from the other side. Often this happens after a long-term power imbalance in the marriage.

If one party has taken full responsibility for the day-to-day financial management of the household, the other person may feel completely uninformed and even embarrassed that they allowed themselves to become so out of touch with the finances. This person desperately needs to have an advocate on his/her side to ensure that their voice is heard and they are educated about what they are entitled to.

The aggressive example is, of course, the opposite. Let's face it, some rather unpleasant behaviors often lead to divorce and create mistrust, anger, and resentment. If you come to the table to negotiate a divorce settlement but your number one priority is to punish the other party, you'll likely get nowhere fast.

What's the point? What's done is done and you will serve yourself well to focus forward and not back. Strive to remember why you fell in love in the first place. Bless the good times you shared – come on, you know there were at least a few – and be committed to moving forward in the most productive, cooperative way possible.

In my own divorce, my ex had been having an affair for nearly a year and I had no idea. The betrayal after 17 years of marriage and 2 children was paralyzing. I felt as though my arms and legs had been brutally torn from my body and everything I knew of who I was disappeared in the instant he uttered the words, "I have something to tell you." I was lost, bobbing in the waters of what remained of my life, certain that drowning was imminent.

Then one day it started to change. About 15 days into my paralysis, the shift began. The sadness and loss gave way to unrelenting thoughts taking me back through the prior year revealing the numerous times his behavior didn't quite make sense. The lies came into focus and I realized that I had not only been betrayed, but a fool as well. And I became angry. I'm not talking about "mad" angry, I'm talking "hunt-you-down-put-a-fork-in-your-face" angry! And it was utterly consuming.

So instead of focusing on my own recovery and being strong for my kids, I found myself stalking his Facebook page, looking for evidence of his misery. I wanted him to be miserable. I found myself outside his apartment, fantasizing about putting a rock through his window and going Carrie Underwood on his car. I fantasized about meeting his girlfriend in a dark alley and going gangsta' on her.

And guess what he was doing. He was being happy with his new girlfriend in his new life. Who the heck did he think he was?! How dare he not be suffering like me!

Here I am 10 years later and realize what wasted energy that was. Do you know what I accomplished?

Here it is. Down and dirty.

1. I was consumed with anger http://bit.ly/2pT1eDe every day and night and I felt miserable. He didn't.

2. I failed to plan for my future http://bit.ly/2pThGmI and my children's. Six months later I was nearly out of money.

3. My health deteriorated. I couldn't sleep, drank too much, and gained 15 lbs.

4. Staying angry meant I wasn't healing. I wasn't looking at MY role in the divorce.

5. My anger had me focused on the past instead of my present and my future. http://bit.ly/2qBjJet

Thankfully I had some very good friends that looked me in the eye and told me that it was time to move on. One friend in particular took my hand one day and said, "Sweetie, he's happy. How much longer are you going to give him the power to determine how you feel? Isn't it about time for you to take your life back and stop letting him be in control?"

Her words hit me like a ton of bricks and I decided then and there to take back control of my life. Things hadn't turned out the way I had planned. But so what? Now it was up to me to write the next chapter of my life. I planned a weekend alone to process my thoughts. I got quiet, listened to some good music, wrote in my journal and made a decision to take a step forward. I closed the book on my marriage and let it go. I wrote him a letter forgiving him and wishing him well.

I didn't send it. It was for me, not him. He had already moved on.

There's no question that divorce can be emotional and uncomfortable to go through. When couples consult with me, I encourage them to move quickly. Once you've decided to divorce, it's not healthy to stay in the limbo land of the process for too long. You both need closure.

#5 – Underestimating Post-Divorce Expenses

No matter which method you choose for your divorce, you will be asked to do a listing of your expenses, the dreaded budget. This is to determine your need for support or ability to pay it, but also to help you plan for your future. Even if you had a budget when you were married, toss it out. You need a new one reflective of your new reality.

Don't get freaked out by the word "budget". I know that when you hear it you think "diet for my money" and that's not the case. A budget is the one and only way you can shift from unconscious spending to conscious choices that will lead to the outcomes you want.

Instead of "diet" think "business plan". That's right, a budget is a "Business Plan for Money" that will guide you to financial success! There, now isn't that better? By the way, a budget is just a list of income and expenses and savings goals. There are TONS of budget tools online and a good financial advisor will be happy to help you get it set up.

In order to accurately estimate your post-divorce expenses, you first have to have a plan. Are you staying in the marital home? Are you planning and able to buy a new home? Do you know how much you can afford? What about the kids? What will be the right situation for them?

This is also a time when you have an opportunity to reinvent yourself. Maybe you sacrificed a career to raise children and now you have an opportunity to go back to school and pursue that long-ago career dream. I see a lot of people around age 50 that think that they're too old to start over.

Hogwash! This is a new age where we can live actively and healthy well into our 90s. The reality of our demographics is that we have a serious shortage of skilled labor so older, experienced, mature workers will continue to be in high demand. I know many, many people who have changed fields over age 50. One of my friends even went to law school after a 30 year career in marketing and is loving her new practice. You can do whatever you put your mind to.

When estimating your expenses, it is critical that you are realistic and don't leave anything out but also don't deliberately inflate the numbers thinking that will get you more support. It only makes you look greedy and unrealistic. Did you include your health care deductibles? How about replacing the roof of your home next year?

What about those things that only come up once a year like draining the pool or having all of your trees trimmed? If you underestimate your expenses by $200 per month, that's $2400 per year. Where are you going to get that extra money? If you're the primary breadwinner, you could end up agreeing to pay alimony that you ultimately can't afford.

In most states, during your divorce process you will have to put this budget into something like a Financial Affidavit or Income and Expense Declaration. There are different names for it in different states. A specialist like a holder of the CDFA®, Certified Divorce Financial Analyst, can help you scrub your affidavit for errors and make sure that you don't leave anything out.

#4 – The settlement doesn't take taxes into effect – AT ALL!

For heaven's sake people, really? We all know that Uncle Sam will dive into our pockets at every opportunity. How could you possibly agree to a settlement without knowing the tax implications? Many people have been stunned to find out that the tax burden on their half of the marital assets is significantly higher than their spouse's making their "half" of the assets worth significantly less than they thought! And DON'T expect your attorney to do this! Attorneys are NOT accountants or financial advisors and a lot of them won't bother to warn you of that. Buyer beware.

I recently met a woman who got the couple's rental property as part of her 50% of the assets. It was valued at $250,000 and had a mortgage against it of $125,000. Her husband received a $125,000 CD as his 50%. A year after the divorce, she decided she couldn't afford to maintain the property and needed to sell.

She then discovered some rather shocking news. Her husband never mentioned, and the attorneys never asked, that he had purchased that property before their marriage for $50,000 which meant that this woman was now going to realize a $200,000 capital gain and owe a whopping $30,000 in taxes. It turns out her half of the assets wasn't as "equal" as she thought.

Every single person embarking on divorce should consult with a tax advisor and preferably one that specializes in the nuances of divorce. CDFA® holders are specialists in all of the financial intricacies of divorce and you would be wise to consult one as early as possible once you are considering divorce. They'll help you ensure that the assets you ask for are really the ones that will help you to live the next phase of your life the way you envision.

Another interesting tax savings opportunity is in deducting your divorce expenses. Did you know you can deduct any fees for your divorce for services that relate to either tax planning or support? For my clients that makes pretty much my entire fee tax deductible.

A seldom-known tax opportunity in divorce is available for qualified retirement plans. IRS Rule 72(t)(2)(c) allows access to retirement assets with no penalty. It works like this. If Husband has a 401(k) and in the divorce gives half to his Wife via QDRO, she has ONE opportunity to remove funds from that account with NO PENALTY no matter how old she is. Any funds taken out will be taxed at ordinary income but this is an often-overlooked way to get a spouse funds for a down payment on a house or to pay off community debts as part of the settlement.

In one case I worked on, the only real assets were 2 401(k) plans, one for each spouse. They were pretty much the same value so we could have just let each party keep their own. However, each of them really wanted to be able to buy a home so their children would be comfortable. I suggested we QDRO 50k from each of their 401(k)s to the other so that they could then take the funds out for down payments. Their response was one that I hear a lot in my practice, "We can do that?" Yes you can!

#3 – Pensions are split 50/50 but no one knows what that really means.

Over and over and over I see divorce decrees that order pensions split 50/50 but no one has any idea what will actually happen.

- When does the non-employee spouse start collecting?

- Is there an option to take a lump sum?

- Will there be a cost of living increase each year?

- What if the employee spouse dies?

- Will it keep paying?

When I ask these questions, no one has ANY IDEA what the answers are? Really?

How can you possibly agree to a settlement where this piece is crucial to your retirement without knowing these details? Again, do not expect attorneys or mediators to be of much help here. It's not their fault, this just isn't their specialty.

Often a pension statement will list a value that is the sum of all the contributions that have been made to the plan as of the statement date. This amount is DRAMATICALLY lower than the actual value of the pension. Don't EVER agree to take another asset instead of your share of the pension based on that value. You MUST get a full present value from a qualified expert. It can make the difference of hundreds of thousands of dollars in your settlement. I'm not kidding.

You'll also want to either have a specialist walk you through the plan documents and guidelines and advise you properly on the division of the plan and what your options are. They are different for every plan and you need all of this information BEFORE you agree to your final settlement, not after.

One of my clients, John, was a City of Phoenix Police officer already receiving payments. As part of his divorce, he assigned 50% of the payments to his ex-wife via QDRO, Qualified Domestic Relations Order. A QDRO is a separate legal document that is required to divide any ERISA regulated retirement plan. I won't go into it here, but entire books are written about QDROs and their pitfalls. Suffice it to be said, it is critically important that you don't wait for the QDRO preparer to answer all of these questions. They MUST be decided during your settlement discussions or your options may end up being significantly limited.

John had been receiving payments for only one year and the couple had been married nearly 30 years. After the divorce was final, it was discovered that the pension plan did not allow an ex-spouse to be listed as a beneficiary which meant that if John died, the ex-wife's pension would stop.

This in itself is not problematic because John could just get a life insurance policy to secure those payments... or not. John had high blood pressure and was a cancer survivor. He was uninsurable and had no other assets to secure the payments. This news was devastating to the ex-wife who was counting on that money to live. What's worse, no one knew these details until AFTER the divorce was final. You don't want to find yourself with those kinds of surprises.

#2 – Keeping a House You Can't Afford

Women especially, tend to get emotionally tied to the family home and often insist on staying. Did they do a budget? Nope. Did they meet with a financial planner? Nope. Then one or two years down the road they run out of cash and realize that they can't sell a window to put food on the table, they can't refinance because they now don't have enough income, and they have no choice but to sell. The selling costs are about 8% of the sale – costs that WOULD have been split 50/50 with the ex-spouse if they had sold as part of the divorce. Stupid, stupid, stupid.

First and foremost, a house is somewhere to live. It does NOT provide any income to support your lifestyle. If you and your spouse lived there for a long period of time, it's highly likely that there is a fairly large chunk of equity trapped in those walls. If you are awarded the home in the divorce, it could be the largest asset in the settlement. Let's assume the home has a market value of $400,000 and there is $300,000 in equity. As marital property, half of that equity is yours, but the other half is your spouse's. So if you keep that home, then a full $300,000 of your settlement will be tied up in that property.

That same money could generate over $15,000 a year in income if it were invested wisely. Not to mention the costs of upkeep and maintenance that will increase the income necessary for you to make ends meet. Various sources estimate the annual cost of home ownership at $834 per month per $100,000. So if you have a $300,000 home, you will need $30,000 per year to keep that house afloat. Included in that number is principal, interest, insurance, maintenance, and taxes. That doesn't include yard care, a pool guy, or replacing the water heater when it fails.

But wait! There's more. The potential tax impacts down the road could be staggering. If you were to sell the house while you are still married, the $300k capital gain would fall under the marriage exclusion of up to 500k and be tax-free. Once you transfer that home into your own name, if you sell it now with a gain of $350k after a couple years of growth, the personal exemption is only $250k so you will owe capital gains tax on 100k of gain or $15,000. Did your attorney remember to take that into consideration in your settlement discussions? Yet one more reason I advocate for a mediated divorce with a financial neutral to help.

So listen, I know "stupid" is not a very nice word and probably ignorance is more accurate. But please, realize what you DON'T know and bring in the right experts for your divorce to make sure that you are SMART and make the best decisions you can with ALL the information! Don't go this alone. As we say at Smarter Divorce Solutions, "You only have one chance to get it right!" Really take the time selecting the right method of divorce and the right professionals to guide your way.

#1 – Drum Roll – The biggest stupid mistake I see is – Losing Money To Save Money

I have yet to find a couple that wasn't determined to keep costs of a divorce as low as possible. Of course, that makes perfect sense. No one wants to spend money frivolously or unnecessarily. Unfortunately, if you have a complex financial situation and/or a long-term marriage, not hiring the right experts can cost you hundreds of thousands of dollars in taxes and mistakes in the settlement.

A couple came to me a year or so ago asking me to help them with their settlement. They were very amicable and had gone to an attorney together – something that makes attorneys very uncomfortable. An attorney's duty is to advocate for one party so they can't work for two people on opposing sides. The attorney let them know this and offered to do their documents for them but made it very clear that he would be unable to give legal advice to either part as it would be a conflict of interest.

The couple thought that could be workable but wondered how they would figure out the property settlement details. "Oh, that's easy," said the attorney. "This is a community property state so we'll just go down each asset and each debt and split each one 50/50." That didn't feel like the right solution for this couple that had been married over 20 years and had a fair amount of financial complexity in their assets.

They knew someone who knew me and retained my services. Just for fun, I did two proposals for them. One was an exact 50/50 split of each item, as the attorney had suggested. The other was my creative settlement solution which was still a 50/50 split on the bottom line.

The total assets of this couple were about $800,000 and in my creative solution, the after-tax amount to EACH of them, was an additional $20,000. That's real money! They paid me about $4,000 for my services and I saved them $40,000 in taxes just by adding some financial intelligence to their settlement.

So as you can see, refusing to pay that extra money for a specialist may cost you a lot more than it will save. If you are unwinding a long-term marriage, you have one chance to maximize all of the financial strategies available to you and attorneys are NOT financial experts. There are a handful of family law attorneys in the country that are also CPAs and CDFAs and have the financial savvy you need but they are few and far between.

If you're going the attorney route and not mediation, here is a list of questions to ask to weed out the less-than-honorable attorneys.

1. *"What percentage of your cases typically go to trial?"*

If the answer to this is more than 20%, BEWARE! That would indicate an overly litigious attorney who doesn't really want you and your spouse to settle but is more interested in racking up the billable hours.

2. *"Will you or someone in your office be helping me prepare an accurate Financial Affidavit?"*

They better answer yes. The financial affidavit will form the basis of all your settlement discussions, child support, and any claim for maintenance. Are you sure your budget is accurate? Have you forgotten expenses that you aren't used to having to pay? Is your budget supposed to reflect current expenses or post-divorce expenses?

3. *"Will you be reviewing my spouse's Financial Affidavit for accuracy?"*

I find that very few attorneys will examine your spouse's affidavit for errors. At the very least, tax withholding is almost always still being calculated as "Married" when it should be "Single". Often I see mistakes in calculating Social Security and I also often see many expenses being double-counted. If no one is looking for these things, it could seriously hurt your case.

4. *If you have been a homemaker - "How soon will I be expected to be back at work and what will the earning expectations be?"*

This is a major, major deal. If you've been a stay-at-home parent for 5 years or more, your skills are outdated no matter what your background is. Be aware that in AZ, you will be expected to be self-supporting very quickly. You'll need a plan. If an attorney tries to tell you that you may get maintenance for more than 5 years, he/she is likely telling you what you want to hear and looking forward to their nice fat case file when you let them fight for an unrealistic settlement.

Other states are more generous with maintenance awards so you need to know your area. In general, California, Illinois, New York, New Jersey, and Pennsylvania still have older maintenance statutes that are more generous but know what your state is like before you interview attorneys.

5. *"Will my spouse and I have an opportunity to try to negotiate a settlement?"*

I find that most attorneys just shuttle written offers back and forth between you and your spouse's attorney without offering you a settlement negotiation meeting. Why? Because they get to bill more for doing all the document write-ups and responses. If the two of you are capable of it, imagine how productive it would be if you both could meet in a room with your attorneys and actually speak to each other on each point. Ask if your attorney is willing to do this.

6. *"Is it ok if I add a Divorce Financial Planner to the team to help me be better prepared for what kind of settlement I should try to get?"*

Again, if the answer to this is anything but "yes", BEWARE! Why would an attorney not want you to have all the information you need? Don't be surprised if your attorney doesn't know anything about CDFAs (Certified Divorce Financial Analysts) and their work. Attorneys are very protective of their billable hours and aren't really interested in delving into the intricacies of the financials of your case. They also are NOT financial specialists and won't really want to do anything other than opt for a 50/50 split on everything which is RARELY the best thing for any couple. A CDFA can save the two of you thousands of dollars in both taxes and attorney fees as I detailed prior.

7. *"I think my spouse may be hiding assets. How will you be sure we know about everything?"*

They should respond to this with assurances that they will be going over several years of tax returns and bank statements to look for any anomalies. However, in order to really know for sure if assets are being hidden or diverted, a forensic accountant or CDFA® is necessary to do the detailed work.

8. *"My spouse owns a business and says it's not worth anything but we live on over $100,000 per year. How will we know the true value of the business and how will the judge know his true income?"*

They should answer that a formal business valuation should be ordered to establish a fair market value of the business. To determine an accurate assessment of annual income, a lifestyle analysis should be done. I've never know an attorney to do these in house. They should be bringing in a CDFA® or Forensic Accountant to establish the basis for an annual income claim.

9. *"I want to keep the house but don't have enough equity to refinance. What are my options?"*

In my experience, most attorneys will say you have 2 options, either refinance the home or sell. Now some will say you can keep the house as long as your spouse will allow you to keep their name on the mortgage. I've never heard them suggest other options. Here are a few that a CDFA® can help you explore.

Continue to own the house jointly for a period of years, usually 3-5, at which point you would either sell or refinance and split the proceeds.

Continue to own the house jointly for a period of years, usually 3-5, but the spouse not living there would receive other assets in lieu of his/her share of the equity. To protect their credit, a clause can be written in that you must provide proof of mortgage payment each month and if at any point the mortgage is more than 30 days past due, the house must be sold.

Continue to own the house jointly and rent it out. A CDFA® can help with the terms of such an arrangement.

10. *"The only assets we have are 401(k) accounts but I need money for a down payment on a house. How can I get cash?"*

As mentioned earlier, pursuant to divorce, if 401(k) assets are transferred to the non-participating spouse via QDRO, Qualified Domestic Relations Order, they have ONE opportunity to remove cash with no penalties. The amount would be taxed as ordinary income but there would be no early withdrawal penalty. This can be a great way to get cash to both parties.

The divorce process is a daunting one. Congratulations on doing the research to ensure yours goes as smoothly as possible and you are protected.

With the resources in this book and the resources on our various websites, you have all the support you need and I wish you peace, success, and happiness in the next phase of your life. I know that right now that seems like a lifetime away but I promise you, there is life on the other side and it's up to you what you make of it. Carpe Diem my friend!

For more help, consider the divorce resources at https://smarterdivorcesolutions.com resources and download our free eBook, "5 Things to Know BEFORE You Decide to Divorce." You only have one chance to do it right.

JULIO BRIONES, CBGS

Personal Crisis Manager, Founder of AnswerMan Specialty Services, LLC.

Email: info@answermanspecialtyservicesllc.com

Website: www.answermanspecialtyservicesllc.com

LinkedIn: www.linkedin.com/in/julio-briones

Facebook: AnswerManSpecialtyServices

Call: (888) 447-4921 / (201) 898-0914

As owner and founder of AnswerMan Specialty Services, Julio Briones consults with a variety of industries including lawyers, addiction treatment centers, government organizations, and a variety of other professionals and services. His company addresses specific needs and issues that in many circumstances cannot be handled in-house, working with clients throughout the United States.

IN A CRISIS? BE PREPARED!

By Julio Briones, CBGS

In life there are times when everything seems to fall apart all at once. Everything will appear to be going well, you are in a good place. Marriage is happy, kids are being kids, life is not perfect, but it is good. Suddenly, you find proof of infidelity; get served divorce papers, get a call from a hospital or the local jail and you are in the middle of a crisis.

Finding yourself in any of these situations is tough enough, but what do you do when you find yourself in one of these circumstances and they begin to compound on each other. You have a couple of choices at this point, you can panic and get overwhelmed by everything that is going on or you can analyze your situation, prepare for what is coming and make a plan for the coming events.

While the most common issue that our clients come to us seeking help with is divorce, they may also have a spouse, child, or other family member that has been arrested. This arrest could be, and usually is, related to drug use and the specter of divorce is in the air.

Their situation could get even more complicated if there are minor children involved or if someone is responsible for the care of an older or developmentally disabled adult. Our goal is to guide our clients and bring them the peace of mind they need to concentrate on their loved ones and we do this by working with our clients to develop a customized plan to get them through the entire process.

Building Your Personal Crisis Toolbox

Once a client reaches out, preparation begins. We do this by working with them to build their Personal Crisis Toolbox. This is what I consider to be the most important part of the process. It all begins with a self-assessment, this is usually completed before we meet with the client in order for them to better gauge where they are and how much help they need.

This is followed by our own comprehensive, non-medical assessment. This assessment allows us to explore fully the needs of the client as well as assess the level of involvement from additional professionals.

The next step is the actual building of the Toolbox. We will let the client know what information they need to gather while we begin to work on their plan. In this plan we will cover a variety of topics depending on their individual circumstances. This will include actions as well as recommendations for additional professionals to seek out, sometimes we will include specific referrals.

You see, most people tend to overlook or underestimate the need for getting prepared and having a plan in place when going through situations such as a divorce. This usually comes about because they simply don't understand how their situations tie together. People will get wrapped up in their own immediate problem, almost as if they have blinders on. Sometimes they are dealing with their own heartache or the pain of the betrayal and ignore what is happening with their children, parents, in-laws, etc.

It isn't easy to deal with divorce at times and by the time they realize that other problems are happening, they get overwhelmed and don't know what to do or how to react. This, often times, leads to them getting in their own way and creating unnecessary obstacles.

The most common obstacle is people fail to understand that their problem isn't as cut and dry as they originally thought. They will believe that because they got divorce papers served, they just need to get an attorney and all will be magically fixed. They will not see how everything else that is going on around them could affect their ability to navigate all their problems and, as a result, will get blind-sided by the reality of the secondary issues. Many times their own shock at having been served the divorce or having to come to terms with the fact that their marriage is over will not allow them to move in a positive direction. They might fail to realize that their children aren't adjusting well, or maybe the divorce is being brought on because the former spouse has been arrested or convicted of a crime.

This could also bring on added guilt because the remaining spouse will not understand fully that they were not responsible directly for the actions of their ex or they might feel as if they are abandoning their spouse in their time of need by moving forward with the divorce. There are many elements that need to be factored into the divorce and just as many complications.

A client was once referred to me that decided to reach out to just because her friend said it would be a good idea to sit down and see if I could help with all that was going on alongside her divorce. She was a little overwhelmed with her whole situation and didn't know what else to do. Her friend had been my client and knew she needed more help than she was getting from her lawyer alone and, also understood the value of getting additional help. When I went to her home for the consultation and assessment, she seemed very unsure about what I could do to help, or even if it would be possible for me to get her on the right track.

At first, it seemed like a cut and dry divorce, her husband of 25 years told her that he did not want to be with her anymore and she could keep the matrimonial home. If this was the situation as a whole, then there was really no need for me to be there, but I knew there had to be more to the story so I decided to keep digging. As we kept talking, it turned out that she had an adult older sister with mental disability in another apartment she owned prior to getting married. Her sister was getting more difficult to manage as she got older and, as a result, the condo association wanted her to vacate the apartment.

Throughout the conversation it also became clear that her son, who was 19 at the time, wasn't handling his parent's divorce very well either and was self-medicating in order to better cope with their constant fighting and this had led to an opioid addiction. If anyone has had to deal with an addicted loved one, this is a big enough challenge to deal with on its own, let alone in the middle of a divorce.

Once we got down to it and completed an assessment, we were able to get everything moving in the right direction. We developed a plan for her and her family, found the right treatment option for her son and began to put the plan into action. I did contact her attorney to explain what I would be doing on behalf of our mutual client, this is important because as professionals dealing with the same client, communication will make certain parts of the process run smoother as we are both working towards the same goal of getting the best possible result for the client.

Working with this client through the assessment process and working with them to develop a plan gave her the understanding of the total circumstances without her getting blindsided by anything, as well as gave her the peace of mind she needed and let her attorney do their job without the additional distraction of a panicking client calling every few hours with questions about circumstances that aren't in the scope of what an attorney would normally handle.

Another common obstacle that people find in their path is generally caused by having unrealistic expectations. In general, these expectations are related to expected outcomes or timeframes for when things should be resolved, more specifically though, they tend to be related to the responsibility of the attorney to take care of situations outside the scope of their law practice.

This could lead to the rapidly climbing price-tag that stereo-typically comes with a divorce. In the United States a divorce can be very inexpensive if it is uncontested. On the other hand, I have seen divorces get so out of hand that the legal fees alone have been in excess of $60,000.00. This is a mostly controllable cost, but is one largely driven up by the parties having emotionally charged or reactionary responses to situations.

Attorneys are highly skilled professionals that invested a considerable amount of time, money and effort into attaining a law degree to be able to assist you with your legal woes. That being said, they will also, on average, bill every 6 minutes. In essence this means your calls to ask who they recommend to help with moving or finding a homecare agency for your parents or what to do about little Jimmy and Sarah acting out could add up very quickly.

Besides the mounting expense, it can also delay progress in your case. While many times there will be a paralegal or some other individual providing assistance to your attorney, there is still a significant amount of work that can only be handled by your attorney. Another important fact to remember is that you are most likely not their only client. This means that the unnecessary interruptions about issues that are not directly related to your legal case could lead to delays in them getting things done on your behalf that should have priority, namely your legal battle.

When I first started my company I received a call from a former colleague who was wondering about my services and what I did exactly. I explained and he referred me to his brother. This situation was a little different from what I was used to at the time because the divorce was the secondary result of more complex problems with addiction and arrest. The client had an adult son who was in the grips of a serious addiction and had been recently arrested for some pretty serious stuff. His wife wanted to wash her hands of the situation and his dedication was more to the son than his wife. He had a time-frame in mind for what should happen as well as how his son's situation should play out.

I went and met with him, this conversation did not go as smoothly as it should have because as we were discussing the details, he kept interjecting his ideas on what he thought should be happening, after all, he watches a lot of court dramas on television and understands "how things really work".

After our meeting and assessment I went back to my office to work on things. I did my due diligence and went back to see him to go over my recommendations and even suggested a couple of attorneys and other professionals that specialized in the specific areas that he needed help with, let him know how I could work with him and his chosen attorney to make everything smoother, I even gave him a brief explanation of what to expect going forward. He still was unable to accept what I told him as being more in line with reality and decided to move on alone.

Having unrealistic expectations can be costly in both time and money. I followed up with my former colleague a few times in the following year just to see how his brother and their family was doing, his brother's delusional expectations led him to disastrous results. He had a detailed plan and chose to ignore it. He hired competent attorney but did not listen to them either. This ended up with him not having a favorable outcome in his divorce and his son getting a much harsher sentence than he should have gotten. Professionals are sought after for a reason, usually for their experience in their chosen field, hiring them to only ignore them completely is a waste of time and resources.

Along with unrealistic expectations, comes the common misconception that many people develop where they think that they can handle all problems on their own; that they don't need to anyone else involved because their lawyer can take care of everything. This is not only a terrible misconception to have, but a mostly foolish one. Attorneys, as mentioned before, are usually very knowledgeable and skilled, this doesn't mean they are one stop shops. Just like you wouldn't call your dentist when your car breaks down and the roof in your house is leaking, you shouldn't rely on your divorce attorney to take care all the secondary problems that you may be dealing with along with your divorce.

The reality is that unless you find yourself in an ideal situation where all parties agreed on every issue before the attorneys get involved, you are going to need help. People don't think about all that is involved when separating intertwined lives. Was the relationship abusive? Are there minor children? Is either person caring for an older relative or an adult relative with a developmental disability? Have alternative living arrangements been made? Are the children exhibiting behavioral issues or showing signs of drug/alcohol abuse? How are the finances going to be handled? Do you know how to manage the household budget?

I had a client that after my initial phone consultation let me know that she could handle things on her own and she couldn't really afford anything beyond her attorney. I understood and let her know to call me if she changes her mind. About 8 months later she calls again, so many problems had compounded on each other that she needed to take a lot of time off work to handle things. This put her in a bad light with her job. She had exhausted all her PTO and still had a considerable amount to take care of.

Since our initial conversation she had been trying to deal with her daughter's inability to accept the divorce. This had led to suspicion of drug use and ultimately an arrest. She was also trying to put into place new living and care arrangements for her older mother who has Alzheimer's disease and is becoming less and less independent very quickly.

The conditions of divorce were being heavily contested and there was an accusation of domestic violence and current concerns about her own safety and the safety of their minor daughter. She was at her wits end and continually calling her attorney for help had cost her $40k up to that point. Had she stayed on as a client, let me help her get organized, prepare and develop a plan, everything would have gone a lot smoother and likely would have saved her financially as well.

Another very common misconception, really more of a myth than anything else, is that if you plan ahead, you are calling bad vibes into your life. The reality is that being prepared has nothing to do with paranoia, mistrust or attracting problems through negative thinking. When you prepare for a personal crisis, you are actually preparing for a variety of circumstances, not just divorce. It is really about having good sense. I suggest everyone have a Personal Crisis Toolbox regardless of what is going on in life because it creates the good habit of organizing and keeping all your important information in a central location.

The core difference between a problem and a crisis is simply the amount of time you have to react to what is going on around you. When you are on the receiving end of a divorce, especially if the announcement of it comes unexpected, the person that filed might have had weeks, months, or longer to prepare for what is coming. If there are children involved and you want custody, for example, they might have the same desire and they might have been gathering the proofs to justify their role as primary caregiver for a lot longer than you have. You might also need to find proofs of joint accounts, private accounts or other financial records. Being prepared ahead of time with some of the more basic information, might save you some headaches down the road.

Being prepared will also help you get ahead of some of the most common pitfalls that most people don't really think about, many times they come as an afterthought when they are trying to deal with the fallout. For example, as mentioned earlier, attorneys generally bill by the hour and in 6 minute increments. This means that those 15 calls you made could end up costing you an extra couple of hundred dollars. Also, your attorney might be great at family issues, but not well versed in criminal; they might refer you to a colleague or try to find the answer for you themselves. This could bring delays in your primary issue and even cost you more than you anticipate. Preparation will prevent a lot of this because you could have had resources in place well ahead of time.

Another common pitfall that comes from lack of preparation is the oversimplification of problems that could lead to inadequate solutions. This underestimation of what is happening could lead to reactionary responses instead of well-planned ones. I had a client that, along with going through a divorce, suspected her daughter was drinking to cope with what was happening. She didn't think it was a big deal and figured if it got out of hand that one place was as good as another for help.

When the situation escalated as a result of a DWI arrest for her daughter, she quickly learned that the world of addiction treatment is more complex than what she imagined it would be. This forced her to make snap decisions and, while the showing of active participation with her addiction did satisfy the prosecution in terms of a more favorable outcome in the courts, them not choosing a proper treatment facility did not result in the right kind of help for the young lady and caused her to ultimately leave college.

When in a crisis you just don't always have the luxury of taking the time to find that ideal solution. It sometimes leaves you at the disadvantage when having to make decisions. Preparation is what fixes that, it is what will bring that peace of mind should crisis strike and allow us to have small amounts of order in the middle of the chaos.

Think of crisis preparation in terms of your home. When shopping for a home you look for a solid structure in a good neighborhood that has low crime rates. As your life in the house continues, you install a security system. This might include an alarm, cameras, panic button, etc. You do this not because you are hoping that someone decided to break into your home, but to be ready should someone make the attempt. This isn't paranoia, it isn't attracting thieves; it is just done for good measure and peace of mind.

A marriage is like a home, you get into it looking for a good structure and to stay for the long term. Having a Personal Crisis Tool Kit and a developed plan is the equivalence of the security system. Just like having an alarm system installed makes good sense at home, having a Personal Crisis Tool Kit and a developed plan makes sense in your life. It will not attract divorce, arrest, or any other crises into your life, but it will make the process smoother if you are prepared.

When in a crisis, my hope is that everyone's goal is to get to the other side of it as smoothly as possible. In the case of a divorce, a lot of this will depend on the amount of time it takes the individual to transition through the pain and grief that comes with ending a marriage, but getting prepared will save you time and bring a little peace of mind to an otherwise chaotic situation.

The less you have to worry about everything that is going on around you, the more time you will have to focus on what really matters the most...you and your family's healing and well-being. I suggest you gather your important documents, if you have children and older relatives, gather theirs as well. Make a set of copies and keep them in a fire-resistant box at home and the originals in a safe deposit box. This will save a lot of aggravation should you suddenly need the information and circumstances prevent you from wondering where the documents are.

At AnswerMan Specialty Services, we serve those dealing with personal crisis; in many cases, more than one at the same time. Our typical clients are going through a variety of situations, in many instances surrounding a divorce, and are feeling lost and overwhelmed. We use our experience and knowledge acquired through many years of helping individuals and families deal with situations such as divorce, arrest, incarceration, addiction treatment placement and helping find the right solution for seniors. All of this is put together to help create the customized plan for each of our clients.

If you are interested in contacting us, visit us on the web at www.answermanspecialtyservicesllc.com.

Call us at (888) 447-4921, (201) 898-0914 or send an email to: info@answermanspecialtyservicesllc.com. We also work with a variety of organizations to provide keynotes and workshops.

MICHELE M. LAWS, CDFA, CFDS, MAFF

Certified Divorce Financial Analyst,

Founder of Divorce Dollars

Email: mlaws@divdollars.com

Website: www.divdollars.com

LinkedIn: linkedin.com/in/divdollarsmichelelaws

Twitter: https://twitter.com/DivorceMlaws

Call: (618) 410-7634

After a complex divorce, Michele felt lead to start her firm Divorce Dollars where she evaluates critical financial situations that are beyond the scope of a family law attorney's expertise.

She feels passionately about empowering her clients to make the most out of their lives and money. Many of them come to her feeling powerless, desperate and discouraged. Her goal is to encourage them, give them hope, educate them on how to become independent, prevent long term regret and take control of their financial lives. She knows the importance of having a divorce team, not just legal counsel.

Michele M. Laws is a registered investment advisor with National Planning Corporation, member FINRA/SIPC and president of SW Wealth Strategies and Divorce Dollars & Sense Corporation. For over 16 years she has been helping individuals make sense of financial changes in their life.

She has a B.A. in Business with a specialization in finance. She received a certifications as a Certified Divorce Financial Analyst (CDFA) from the Institute of Divorce Financial Analysts, a Certified Financial Divorce Specialist (CFDS) from the Financial Divorce Association and a Master Analyst of Financial Forensics (MAFF) from the National Association of Certified Valuators and Analysts.

EMPOWER YOURSELF

By Michele M. Laws

Mindset and Money

The first moment after the divorce papers were filed, what crossed your mind? Were you asking yourself things like, "Where do I start? How do I know if I'm going to be okay financially? How am I going to be able to afford to pay my bills? Who will get what property? How can I make sure the settlement will be enough for me? Can I afford the house? How do I know my spouse is being truthful about our money? How will I know if my spouse is hiding money from me? "

These questions may sound familiar to you?

While you are already feeling the emotional roller coaster, you also have this financial mess about which to worry. You may be anxious and unsure of your next step and knowing what is best for you. You are not alone. Once a decision to divorce is made, all sorts of uncertainties will come to mind. These questions are asked by most people when going through a divorce. When you have the right divorce team, many of these issues can be answered and can put your mind at ease. Constructing the right panel of professionals will help you strive towards a stress-free divorce. **You only have one opportunity to get it right.**

Where to Start

You're probably wondering what a divorce team is, why you need one, and where to start creating a team. Remember the old saying, "You don't know what you don't know"? Well, it is absolutely true in divorce. You will need assistance in figuring out how to proceed. Most divorces are more complicated than just child visitation and dividing a few bank accounts. It is imperative to have a team of experienced professionals in whom you can trust to guide and support you through the process.

Whether you desire the divorce or your spouse has filed, decisions will need to be made. Each state and county may have a different process to follow, but they will all be similar in nature. Paperwork will have to be filed with the courts, and a judge dissolve your marriage, regardless of the procedure you choose for the divorce.

The manner in which you are choosing to obtain your divorce will dictate some of who your team members are. There are a number of different alternatives you can use to get the actual dissolution finalized. It could be as simple as filing the documents yourself, you could sit with a mediator to guide you on the decisions, or you may need your own attorney to protect your interests. Sometimes you may start with one type of divorce action, such as a collaborative divorce which will include two attorneys, a financial expert, a mental health professional, and other needed specialists, but be unable to come to necessary agreements. At that point, you will each have to start over, get new attorneys and experts, and begin the legal process through the courts.

Typically, if you have had a hard time agreeing on matters during the marriage, it will likely be even more difficult to compromise on those same issues during divorce proceedings. Only a small percentage of divorce cases go to trial, but a good number of cases typically involve two attorneys negotiating for their clients. Only you know the route you feel most comfortable taking and what your spouse may be most receptive.

At the onset of divorce, you should begin taking a financial assessment of what you have. If you have not dealt with the family finances, this may send you into a panic mode. The easiest thing to do is to start collecting any documentation regarding the finances. Examples of vital records you will need are the past five years of tax returns including: all attachments such as W-2's and 1099's; documents of all loans including closing statement and balance; bank and credit card statements; all investment, retirement, and pension statements; one year of pay stubs; employer benefit books or contract; recent credit reports; and life insurance information including death benefit, type of insurance, and cash value, if any. If you or your spouse have an interest in a business, you should look for past five years corporate tax returns with all attachments such as K-1's and 1099's, balance sheets, profit and loss statements, business agreements and bank and credit card statements. This list of items will give a preliminary to the financials of the marriage. Depending on your particular situation, a variety of insight into other documents may be required. It is best to make a copy of these documents before giving them to your divorce team professionals.

The Process

As you get the process rolling, it is also a good time to develop a different mindset. It is easy to get wrapped up in the emotions and the idea of "winning." In divorce, nobody wins. Everyone loses something. Divorce can be very emotional for all parties involved, especially if you have children. It is easy to obsess about the toxic issues that happened in your marriage, but this will only block and prevent you from making the right decisions for your future. If you find that it is very difficult to develop a healthy mindset, a counselor or therapist should be sought out for your divorce team. The majority of the clients I see in my office will see a mental professional to help them process the emotions concerning the ending of their marriage.

Depending on the circumstances that led to the divorce, there may be other issues to examine as well. *It is imperative to keep the right perspective and focus on what is most important.* So, what is most important to you? Have you given it any thought? Is it best to negotiate everything together to save fees and avoid a long drawn out process? Is it having enough money to support you and your children in the lifestyle you are accustomed to? Is it making sure you stay in the same house? Is it the fear of running the finances? Is it how divorce will financially and emotionally impact you and your children? These topics will be very difficult to think about, especially in the early stages. *However, if you do not know what is most important, it will be very difficult to determine what you need and who is a must on your divorce team.*

Decide Your Team

Your divorce team should be individuals who will assist you based on what is most important to you. While divorce is often about two issues, children and money, it is shocking the number of people who do not realize the various professionals and experts available to assist them in addition to their attorney. Divorce is different for everyone. Depending on the dynamics of your family and the complexity of your divorce, various professionals and experts may be needed on your team.

While this chapter will mention several types of professionals, its primary focus is to educate you on the importance of a financial team and ways they can serve you. This will be the team that will create a strategy plan for you.

If you are like most parents, your children will be the first thing that comes to mind once a divorce is imminent. You will wonder how they are going to be supported financially. How often will you see them? What will be process will be for their schooling, their religious upbringing, and even their scheduled activities? Children are served best is if you and your spouse can agree on how you will jointly parent them. If you are unable to agree on the issues surrounding your children, an expert may be needed called a Guardian ad Litem (GAL). This individual will speak for your children on the issues upon which no agreement is reached. The expert will typically be chosen by the respective attorneys or appointed by the court.

The first professional you will usually seek for advice is an attorney or a financial expert. It is essential to find an attorney who concentrates on family law and a financial professional that specializes in divorce. You would not ask your mechanic to fix electrical problems in your home, so why would you ask your estate attorney to file your divorce? Also, you would not ask your plumber to fix your roof, you would not ask your investment advisor or accountant to help with the financial analysis of your divorce. While each individual may be very competent at their particular profession, they typically will not have the specialized education and knowledge needed for divorce analysis.

There are many financial experts, and each of whom focus in distinctive areas. If you are seeking a financial expert first, you should find someone who is a certified divorce financial analyst (CDFA). A CDFA professional blends the expertise of a financial planner and an accountant. This expert brings an innovative and creative approach to divorce which has been previously missing in traditional divorce negotiations. Each will have specialized education to conduct the appropriate financial analysis regarding the financial aspects of divorce. Their role will be to assist the attorney with the financial portion of the divorce.

Attorneys are experts at law, not finance. Even if your attorney has some financial background, they will not be allowed to testify on your behalf. The CDFA can help save time and money especially in the beginning while everyone is trying to get a clear picture of the assets, debts, and income streams. *You must obtain a good understanding of these matters, or financial pitfalls could occur if assets or income is overlooked or not understood.*

Develop Your Strategy

The first items that will need to be analyzed are the financial documents representing the time of your marriage. All assets and debts will need an assigned value in order for them to be divided. The income of both the husband and wife will need to be determined as well as the expenses so that support can be calculated, if needed. Your attorney and divorce financial analyst will seek basic documents such as tax returns, life insurance, 401k, pension, and bank and investment statements. They may also ask for the corporate financial books if you or your spouse are business owners. During the initial review of these documents, various inconsistencies or additional income streams, assets, or debts may be uncovered. Each will require additional clarification or investigation.

If all that sounds overwhelming, you are not alone! Many will read the paragraph above and become paralyzed at the next step. Anxiety often begins right here. That is why it is important to construct the right team so you can work through your divorce wisely. There is a step-by-step process for each portion of the divorce. Sometimes, the steps may proceed quickly and other times very slowly. ***Each case is different, but it is important to have realistic expectations. It is in your best interest to be open minded with your divorce team and look at the big picture, especially with the financials.***

Your financial expert will make the attorney aware of what is contained in the financials. While the attorney will review the documents, they typically do not spend as much time in the details as the CDFA will, especially if they are dealing with complex assets. All experts used in your case will complement your attorney, not replace them. The attorney will direct financial experts as to which scenarios and settlement offers they would like to see calculations based on what is contained in the financials. The financial analyst will prepare numeric analysis and reports to support the attorney's position for your case. These reports will show the hardship or surplus of income as well as the financial effect of the asset division. *Attorneys will use these analysis reports to finalize settlement ideas for their clients.*

The type of analysis completed will be different with each and every case. The scope or subject matter in which a CDFA can support your attorney is vast. One of the most common methods of support is to show data of the financial effect of a proposed settlement. Each scenarios will have a short and long term financial effect. So, what does this mean for you? It shows if the amount of the marital portion and amount per month proposed will be sufficient for you. Sometimes, a little more per month can make ends meet for one spouse but barely affect the other.

A projection of income and net worth will help evaluate if a settlement is equitable for both spouses. This does not necessarily mean an equal amount to each of you. You should take note that not all assets are created equal. What appears on the surface may not necessarily be correct. In many cases, an attorney may only be looking at one aspect, such as the division of the assets, but would not be aware of the tax impact of those particular assets.

They may not consider the cost of the asset such as the monthly liability payments, the cost of upkeep, and where those funds will come from. The tax impact of support may not have been taken into consideration. While child support is not taxable, spousal support is taxable to the person receiving the support and deductible to the person paying it. The spouse receiving the support may be expecting to receive one amount, but after the impact of taxes, may only receive a 2/3 of it.

Needless to say, if someone receives a 1/3 less than they need to meet monthly expenses, they may deplete all their assets or incur debt to make the payments. This can create a negative domino effect that may have been avoided if the proper analysis had been completed. *This type of forecasting helps reduce the financial uncertainty of the future.*

There is tremendous power in the financial forecasting analysis of the settlement. An example that comes to mind is a case I testified in four years ago. My client was the wife, and they had three children. The husband was a high income wage earner and a business owner, so the numbers on paper appeared to be substantial. The financial position the husband's attorney presented in court appeared to be equitable at first glance, and the support payments appeared to be sufficient to maintain the lifestyle for the wife and children. However, once the settlement numbers were calculated, it showed she would have to sell or foreclose on the family home by year six based on his suggested division of assets and the support he would pay. The analysis of the numbers showed he would grow a substantial net worth while she would slowly slide into the poverty level.

We showed a different division and support scenario to the judge which allowed both parties to maintain their lifestyle, meet stated expenses, and continue to build their net worth. When the judge gave her final order, it was very close to our financial position. The projection showed that the support amount the husband was willing to pay did not serve the family for that period of time. It also showed the percentage of assets he was willing to give her would provide her enough liquid assets to pay expenses during times of shortfall which later forced a foreclosure or sale.

This illustrates the importance of understanding the short and long term impact of the financials as a whole. There may be financial benefits and consequences of keeping one particular asset over another. The division amount may seem appropriate, and the support amount may appear to be enough to cover expenses by themselves. When you look at the overall effect of them together, the settlement may not be in the best interest of both spouses. *It is important to project the financial health of both parties based on the assets given to each and the support that will be paid.*

A commonly overlooked item that would greatly affect the long term impact of the settlement is the need for life insurance on the spouse paying the support payments. If this person passes away, the stream of support ends. A small amount per month for a life insurance premium would give a great peace of mind the person receiving support. It is best if the spouse receiving the support owns the policy. This would ensure the premium payments are made so that the policy does not lapse, cancelled or had beneficiaries changed.

Another typical analysis performed to support the attorney's position is calculating the true income of a spouse. A tax return will not show the families true cash flow. Taxable income is the gross income from all sources minus any deductions or exemptions for that year. Cash flow is the amount of money you have available to pay expenses. The tax returns will show deductions such as contributions made into an HSA, charitable contributions, and retirement account contributions all of which would be considered part of annual cash flow.

The cash flow will include all funds and compensation received by the individual from employment income, corporate income, benefits of an employer or corporation, and other gifts. If we rely solely on someone's taxable income, we would be missing cash flow from corporate distributions, economic benefits, and other amounts paid such as 401k contributions as these would not appear on a tax return.

Someone's income or lack thereof is very important to determine the support needed and the financial ability to pay support. The economic benefits received may be annualized and considered part of the cash flow total. This type of compensation would be imputed as income to the individual who received it.

Imputed income is income that is "credited" to that spouse. While this spouse may not actually be earning that amount of income, they may have earned it in the past or received the compensation in another form. Your attorney and the courts will decide what portion of the imputed income or if all of it can be used for the purpose of calculating support. Your team will assist you in uncovering the value of the compensation your spouse receives. In the corporate world, executives and business owners can be compensated in creative ways. It could be in the form of different memberships such as country club or elite associations, car leases or payments, stock options, or even travel benefits.

Your spouse could have also received compensation in the form of bonuses such as sign on, annual, and sales driven benchmarks. Many executives receive reimbursements for expenses they may have paid or have other career assets which will have a value.

One may be realizing at this point that it makes complete sense to calculate some projections on the assets. You may have even completed financial planning with an advisor in the past and have heard similar things. What is not understood is why your spouse's income matters or why yours means anything during the divorce. Unless you are both roughly earn the same income, have the same expenses, or each have an inherited trust account somewhere, you will more than likely be analyzing your incomes. **While you may not "divide" income in the divorce, it may be redistributed between the two of you so that each of you can attempt to remain in the same lifestyle you had during the marriage.**

Many individuals have been previously married or they were married later in life, so they acquired assets prior to their marriage. The line between marital and non-marital property may not always be clear. Depending on your jurisdiction, the non-marital assets could be handled in different ways. The income generated from those assets are also handled differently. You would need a CDFA to calculate the accurate percentage of each within the asset. Due to market conditions, especially in the last seventeen years, the market downturn could have had a large effect on non-marital portion of the account balance. This calculation is not a simple subtraction method. Various lump sum assets may also need to be traced back to the origination source to determine the validity of the non-marital claim. Martial contributions can erode a non-marital assets in a number of ways.

Last year, I had a case in which the wife was the higher wage earner and owned the savings coming into the marriage. During the period of 8 years, she contributed larger percentages into the account than she did prior to the marriage. She was quickly eroding the non-marital portion of the retirement account. Quick math indicated that she lost a greater share of her non-marital portion in a year of market downturn. Precise calculations showed the opposite. In one account, she received 7% more than she would have in the simple subtraction method of just subtracting the balance on the day of the marriage from the current balance.

Calculations for her second account, revealed she received 18% more! The details of the numbers are very important. Without the correct members of your team, this type of situation would have been typically overlooked.

Your CDFA can assist you in preparing the financial statement required by the courts which will detail your income and expenses as they are today and how you project them into the future. I cannot stress enough how important it is to get assistance with this document. I have NEVER seen a financial statement prepared correctly by a client. I have only seen them somewhat correctly prepared by a law firm, but even some of these showed mistakes. *If you do not know the correct way to prepare the financial statement, mistakes made could jeopardize future support.*

Examples of common mistakes made in this document are the number of paychecks per year, the payroll deductions, and the amount for child expenses. I also see both the husband and wife double count the same expense for themselves and their children. Attorneys are going to look for glaring errors and mistakes, not review with a fine tooth comb. This is the document your attorney and the judge will be using at to determine your current lifestyle and if you need any financial assistance from your spouse. *Likewise, this same document will reveal the amount of income you have left each month after all expenses and taxes are paid to determining your ability to pay support.*

Both attorneys and the judge will want to know how income was spent during the marriage and how it is anticipated to be used for future costs. They also want to see the amount spent on the children's behalf as well as discretionary and non-discretionary expenses. We all know it will cost more to run two homes, but only certain expenditures will increase. There will often be dispute regarding overstated expenses. Sometimes, spending will increase with the intent of showing inflated expenses. This type of ruse will inaccurately show a greater need for support or less disposable income.

How would anyone know if the financial statement is accurate or realistic? There is always a marital standard of living and a necessary amount to sustain it. We need to have a handle on past expenditures to determine if future expenses are realistic, intentionally inflated, or even just a made up number. We would need to construct a comprehensive report called a lifestyle analysis. This report shows a 3-5 year historical income and expense analysis using all known sources of income and spending of the family. Without this, it is merely a guess. This is similar to the financial statement of income and expenses required by a court jurisdiction but reconstructs the family's financial life. *This lifestyle analysis is often used to determine the amount of child and spousal support to be paid in your case.* Once completed, it will serve as a verification for the judge as to the lifestyle created in your marriage. It will show the trend of spending and how much income had been available to cover those expenses.

I had a case a few years ago in which the husband was my client. He made a greater percentage of the income but also had more expenses. They had four teenage children; she worked part time and lived in a home without a mortgage. An analysis of income and expenses showed that her need was not even as great as the guideline showed in that state. If he paid the guideline, which is what the wife was asking, she would have a surplus every month.

The husband, on the other hand, would be running at a substantial monthly deficit and be forced to liquidate investments just to pay her. On paper, it looked like she needed the income if you looked only at their net incomes and her "guess" on expenses. When it was analyzed, it showed she double counted and inflated expenses and over-withheld on her taxes to show a lower net; Therefore, she needed much less support than she was asking.

The lifestyle analysis will show spending behavior patterns of both the husband and wife. You can only do two things with money - save it or spend it. It will show if one or both of you were savers or spenders. If you were savers, then we should find all contributed funds within the known bank or investment accounts. If certain amounts cannot be found, money may have been directed to an account you are unaware. If you were spenders, it will show the type of items you were buying, expenses you were incurring and where they were from.

There will be a trend or disconnect when compared to the current spending pattern. Spending patterns may uncover additional assets or streams of income that you were previously unaware of. An example could be employer reimbursement checks. If they are not found deposited into an account, they may have been diverted into an unknown account or just cashed and kept. The checks for reimbursements would need to be traced and the expenses separated in the lifestyle analysis from the family's expense. *It is during this type of analysis in which an affair, hidden income, or hidden assets are discovered.*

I recently had a case in which the spouse started having SIDS (Sudden Income Deficiency Syndrome) shortly after the divorce was filed. A four-and-a-half-year analysis was completed to show his income went down by over 60% while his expenses increased by 30%. You do not need to be a math major to realize something deceptive was going happening.

They lived separately during most of this time, so the lifestyle analysis showed a clear trend before and during the proceedings. After reviewing bank records, it became clear he choose to underreport his income while increasing his discretionary spending. The unreported income coincided with the divorce proceedings. The type of discretionary spending showed he had significant free time on his hands, a substantial amount of disposable income, and was not working very much. All the while, he was claiming he was broke and could not pay his wife temporary support due to the decrease in income.

The Investigative Members

If you are a family that has become accustomed to living a comfortable lifestyle but suddenly the income barely pays the bills, you are probably suspecting foul play. On the other hand, if your spouse is a high income earner, you may not even realize funds are missing. If your marriage has been breaking down for some time, you may be suspicious. During divorce, I often hear the statement, "They are hiding money", and the feeling is usually correct. If you know money should be somewhere, and you cannot locate it, you will need an expert called a forensic analyst to assist in analysis such as reconstructing income, tracing of assets, and an audit of activity to determine what has transpired.

Forensic analysis is the investigation of people and money. It is not enough just to suspect someone is hiding an asset or diverting income; you have to prove it. It is rare that one would admit to this type of dishonesty during the divorce. Often times in a case of business owner who is filing for divorce, they may have been "planning" for it for some time. This owner may have done things such as create fake payroll, "write checks" that are not cashed, manipulate business assets, fabricated debts, underreport income, or over report expenses.

If someone had been "planning" for the divorce, they may have also moved accounts to another bank so that the spouse could not see the transactions. They may have had a portion of the income direct deposited into a secret account. Once the marital bank records are viewed, this income diversion becomes clear. A pattern of activity will emerge, inconsistencies will begin to develop, and financial holes will materialize such as unreported income or missing assets.

This analysis may prevent dissipation of marital assets after they are detected or aid the recovery of them. It may also show a level of income that records may not reflect otherwise. ***Forensic analysis is understanding the cash flow of all income and asset sources.***

Assets and debts have a definitive beginning and an end. Sometimes, the end is the current balance. A timeline needs to be constructed to see when accounts were opened and closed as well as when assets were purchased. If lines of credit were opened during that time, tracing where funds went, what the disbursement of funds purchased and how the debt service payments were made is constructed. There are several methodologies to determine hidden income or assets if your spouse refuses to submit required discovery to your attorney or the courts.

This type of analysis will be very time intensive and could get very expensive. If it comes down to this, it is important to determine if the analysis will be worth it. If a forensic analyst is used, you may also need a forensic accountant. While an analyst is looking for patterns of activity and analyzes the dates within, a forensic account will audit the books and apply accounting methods within the analysis. This is another layer of forensic methodology. This expert would be combining their accounting skills and investigative skills to analyze the financial information. They will examine and evaluate using accepted accounting standards.

Deception can be hard to prove without a financial expert. I experienced a very complex divorce myself in 2008. During divorce litigation, many games can be played. Spouses create fake contracts, begin undisclosed businesses, stash hidden money, and create false debt knowing it can be difficult to prove. Others play the shell game and move funds between numerous accounts, most which are undisclosed to the court.

Spouses and their attorneys may use ploys of stall tactics and temporarily reduce income in order to distract from what they were really doing. I recognize through my own divorce where the lack of fairness can present itself and the importance of a financial analysis. My own experience was similar to the situations I am describing. Unfortunately, I did not have a divorce team. The result left me with too little money for a new secure beginning. *I knew after my own experience, if it happened to me, it was happening to countless others. That was when I felt lead begin an analytics business to help others facing the same circumstances.*

Special Team Members

If you or your spouse owns, operates, or invests in a business, it will need to have a value assigned to it. This value is assessed by mean of a business valuation. A closely held business is a prime example of a complicated asset. The value must be calculated in order to determine how it will be divided. At times, an accountant can perform a business valuation but some are not trained in this specialty. If they are not, you will need a certified valuator on your team. The term valuator and appraiser tend to be used interchangeably but both experts offer opinions of a business's value.

There are times when some of the assets need to be appraised and become part of the actual value of the business. Even if the business was owned prior to the divorce, the non-owner spouse may still have an amount of financial interest in the business. The divorce analyst, forensic specialists, and the business valuator would need to collaborate in order to come up the marital and non-marital portions. They would also work together to ensure the "real" numbers are used if there was any suspected fraud or deceit in the business books.

All real estate property should have an appraisal completed. There are times a real estate appraisal will be conducted within a business valuation. One example of this would be if you own rental property. This particular piece of property not only has a value as the brick and mortar asset, it also has a value based on the income it produces. Depending on when your property was purchased, the value may have increased significantly. The real estate property most couples own can be the largest asset they have other than a pension plan.

Your New Beginning

After the final papers have been signed, there is still more to do. You will need someone to prepare a financial checklist. Your CDFA professional or a financial advisor will be the team member to help formulate this list. This team member will be your assistant to help you finalize all that is required of you in your marital settlement agreement or final order.

You will need to finalize things like changing the names & beneficiaries on accounts, debts, and titles of the various assets you were awarded. If you received an IRA or other investment account, you will need to determine how you would like to invest it. If you received a 401k, something called a QDRO will need to be entered so that you can receive the asset in your name. This will take both the financial advisor and the attorney to complete. This is also a time you may be able to take a special distribution from the retirement account, pay the taxes, and avoid the 10% if completed correctly.

If life insurance was part of your settlement agreement, rates will need to be researched on your ex-spouse for proper coverage to cover the stream (s) of support. Once you have completed your follow up list, you will be ready to discuss your financial goals for your future. You will need a new team to help you in the new chapter of your life. Some divorcees keep the financial professionals they had during the marriage, but many find new ones.

A financial advisor should be the first contact. They can assist you in putting together a financial plan for you and determine what is needed to achieve your new goals. The financial plan will include goals such as retirement, college expenses, and major purchases.

It will be a comprehensive analysis similar to the divorce analysis but will only forecast based on your goals. The financial advisor will continue to help monitor on a regular basis to make sure your goals continue on track while making necessary adjustments along the way. Over time, your life may change, and this expert will help guide you with future financial decisions.

An accountant will be necessary to assist you looking at your new financial tax picture, calculate and file estimated quarterly taxes if necessary, and assist in the filing of the final marital tax return, if needed. In the divorce settlement, you may have received various assets which will have tax consequences. You may also need to assess what you need to do in order lower your tax liability.

A new estate attorney will be needed to update any will and trust work based on the new financial picture. Be sure to reclaim old copies of legal documents and destroy them so there is no confusion as to which is in effect. It is extremely important to confirm all beneficiary designations on your property and assets.

Divorce can be devastating. You may experience almost every emotion there is, on the same day. As the proceedings come to a close, hopefully you will be able to find some peace after the storm. If there are feelings of anger, hurt or bitterness towards your ex, this may be a time you are able to make the choice to forgive them. As you continue on your journey to rebuild your new beginning, you will continue to feel more confident with the *"new you."* You will be a stronger, more inspired individual than you were when it all began. At some point, you may even be able to see the lessons in the heartache and know there was always a greater plan.

If you feel like the whole process of divorce is too overwhelming, then call (618) 410-7634 and book your own *"60 Minutes Financial Strategy Session."* After this session, over the phone or in person, you will feel empowered for a new beginning. In addition, you can obtain our free reports, *"Costly Mistakes In Divorce"* and "What You Shouldn't Leave Home Without" at http://divdollars.com/free-resources

"For I know the plans I have for you, "declares the Lord,
"plans to prosper you and not to harm you, plans to give you hope
and a future. Jeremiah 29:11

DOMINIQUE CALLINS, ESQ.

Family Law Attorney

Attentive Law Group, PLLC

Email: dcallins@attentivelaw.com

Website: www.attentivelaw.com/dominique-callins

LinkedIn: www.linkedin.com/in/dominique-callins

Twitter: https://twitter.com/DACallinsESQ

Call: (703) 444-0055

Dominique Callins is an attorney with Attentive Law Group, PLLC, in Ashburn, Virginia, where she serves as the Family Law Section Leader. For nearly a decade, Dominique has provided clients with competent, efficient and zealous legal representation during a most vulnerable and personal time in family life.

She is dedicated to developing practical legal solutions, while preserving important family relationships. Her extensive experience includes divorce, child custody and visitation, spousal support and alimony, child support, high net-worth asset division, military divorce, support enforcement, international child abduction.

After law school, Dominique served as a judicial law clerk in both trial and appellate courts in Virginia. Prior to her legal career, Dominique was a public school teacher. As a teacher, she gained experience directly counseling children and parents through family transitions, understanding proper and effective communication between children and adults—which has helped shape her career in family law.

She is a graduate of Florida A&M University, summa cum laude, and the College of William & Mary, Marshall-Wythe School of Law.

DIVORCE: FOCUSING ON THE THINGS THAT MATTER:

By Dominique Callins Esq.

As a divorce attorney, I meet very good people at the very worst time in their lives. Intelligent, professional, successful people often come to me as inarticulate, irrational balls of massive emotion. Why should anyone expect differently? Divorce can be one of the most the most emotionally vulnerable times in a person's life.

Because divorce is such a vulnerable time, too often the last consideration is the cost of the divorce process. To be clear, clients regularly ask about the hourly rate and the amount of an up-front retainer. They are often too focused on those initial numbers. What I am referring to is the accrual of fees on a day-to-day basis: telephone calls and email exchanges, document production, hearings, trials and preparation time. Clients are often not aware how interactions with their attorneys and choices in strategy affect the cost of a divorce.

In my work, I encourage clients to rethink divorce as a transition period and a path to their next, better chapter in life. It's so important that people come out feeling whole and empowered. To get to this place, the focus must be on the things that matter: you, your children, and your financial stability.

A good attorney should discuss with you not only your options, but also the costs associated with each option. Your future-ex may have given you every reason conceivable fault-basis for a "scorched earth" divorce campaign. But if the only gain at the end is half of a $1,000.00 bank account balance, scorched earth may not be the best option financially or emotionally. Freedom always comes with a price. However, when the price is so high that it outweighs the benefit of freedom, it is time to rethink your plan.

So, how do you avoid a costly divorce and still focus on the things that matter? I break it down into 4 important considerations.

1. ***Hourly Rate Isn't Everything: Don't choose your attorney based solely on his or her fees.***

Choosing the right attorney is an important step on the road to your divorce. Your relationship with your attorney is one of the most intimate of your life. Unlike the guy/gal you married and are now divorcing, this time be more selective!

Notice I said the *right* attorney, not the "best" attorney. The title of "best" is conferred based upon subjective criteria. One person may consider her attorney "the best" because the attorney was super aggressive during her husband's cross-examination; another person says his attorney is "the best" because they settled the case without going to court. As you can see in these examples, what constitutes the best really depends upon your goals for the process.

How do you know which attorney is right for you?

a. Determine your goals

In order to determine whether an attorney is right for you, you have to know what you want out of the process. Are there significant assets to be divided in your case, such as houses, investment accounts or businesses? Do you and your spouse see eye-to-eye on custody of your children? Are you a victim of domestic abuse and need physical as well as financial protection? Do you and your spouse agree to separation and want to resolve your matters outside of a courtroom?

These are among many questions you should ask yourself about your circumstances. Sketch an outline of what you are hoping to achieve through the process, of the issues that you know need to be addressed, and/or of specific questions you may have.

But Dominique, you may say, *I don't even know what to want, let alone what I want.* My response? It's ok. There are seminar and webinar programs all over the country available to help people learn about divorce law and their rights. Investigate what seminar programs are available in your area. These programs are designed to provide general information; don't expect them to address all of the concerns you may have about your specific circumstances. But the programs do help educate you regarding your general rights, as well as your options for trial and alternative dispute resolution.

b. Get recommendations for attorneys

Now that you have an idea about what you want, you are ready to talk to an attorney. *One problem*, you say: *I don't know any divorce attorneys.* First, congratulations! Second, it's ok. Even if you personally do not know any divorce attorneys, chances are you know someone who does. Ask for recommendations from family members or close friends who may have gone through the process. Talk to a service professional you trust, such as your accountant, realtor or family doctor. An excellent referral source may be a lawyer you use for different matter: your personal injury attorney or your real estate closing agent.

When all else fails, you can always "google it." Look for divorce attorneys who practice those who primarily practice family law and in your local area. The internet is inundated with attorneys claiming to be "the best" this or the "top ten" that. While commendations are nice, they are not always the helpful in predicting your experience with the attorney. A personal referral is the better route, if you can take it.

c. Ask questions

Because you will have already done some background research on the divorce process in your state, you can go into your consultation armed with your goals—and with questions about how to achieve them. Remember, the seminar you will have attended provided you with general information. Meeting with an attorney gives you the opportunity to learn how that general information may be applied to the facts of your case.

An attorney should be prepared to advise you regarding the general state of divorce law. That is her job. However (speaking from experience), a good attorney is invigorated when meeting with a client clearly armed with a plan and with questions! It is indicative of an individual who will be fully engaged in the process. This allows the attorney to advise you specifically regarding how and whether your goals may be achieved.

It also gives you the opportunity to observe the attorney's approach, and process whether his demeanor and approach is consistent with your own. Is the attorney listening to you or just talking at you? Are they talking to you about options, or indicating that the only way to get what you want is to go to trial? Is she insisting on a "scorched earth" approach despite you telling her you and your spouse agree to mediation? You are looking for an attorney who can align with your goals and you approach. When that doesn't happen, you can end paying too much in the end, either in unnecessary litigation expenses or as a result of having to hire a new attorney to clean up the mess!

d. Interview more than 1

Just as in personal relationships, you should be wary of the "love at first sight" syndrome in divorce consultations. I am not advocating for ignoring your intuition or "gut" feeling— people often do so to our detriment. I am suggesting you test your "love" to ensure it is pure. By that I mean simply, interview more than one attorney if at all feasible.

Divorce and family law attorneys usually charge a fee for their consultations, which can range anywhere from $100 to $500 per hour. So, I understand it may be an expensive proposition to interview multiple attorneys. However, considering the average contested divorce in the United States costs $15,000.00 to $20,000.00[1], the cost of a consultation may be worth ensuring the right fit.

e. Don't be intimidated—or suckered in—based on the amount of the fee

In divorce and other family law cases, an attorney may charge either a flat fee or an hourly fee.

Flat fees are usually what they sound like: you pay a single fee for the agreed legal service. On its face, the flat fee sounds appealing, right? Your legal fees are capped and you know exactly what they are. Depending on the circumstances, this may in fact be a good option. However, it is important that you read the fine print on that engagement contract. Flat fee arrangements are often very limited in scope. Your fee may include your attorney's appearance at the divorce trial, but not include conducting the discovery necessary to prepare for that trial. Or the agreement may limit the number of revisions to a draft separation agreement before incurring additional fees. These are just a few examples.

An attorney charging an hourly fee determines her hourly rate based on a host of factors: years of experience, caliber of experience, local market competition, overhead costs, subjective service value. Her engagement agreement should state everything to which her hourly rate applies. If it does not, ask: do you charge for travel time, administrative tasks, reviewing emails and/or text messages? Is there a different fee for work performed by an associate or a paralegal, and what is the fee?

A lawyer's fee is not necessarily indicative of the quality of a lawyer, but rather of the value the *lawyer* has placed on his services. It is a myth that an expensive lawyer is always the best, or that a cheaper lawyer is the worst. So, don't believe another prevailing myth: that you can't afford a good lawyer. The *right* lawyer is always going to be worth it, and choosing the wrong lawyer can be very expensive.

Just like with every other aspect of your life, it is advisable to stay within a reasonable budget when it comes to attorney fees. One of the best ways to ensure that your attorney is not the sole winner at the end of this process is to follow this guidance, and choose the *right* one.

2. *The Cost of Crying in Your Attorney's Office: Using other resources during your divorce*

So, you have found the perfect attorney, gathered together and paid your retainer fee—what next? Well, use up that hefty retainer fee, of course! Call your attorney every chance you get, give him a blow-by-blow of what your spouse told you, what you told your spouse, what the kids said to you, and so forth and so on. When your attorney calls you to discuss discovery strategy, use this opportunity to remind him of all the reasons you are getting a divorce to begin with, because doesn't he remember what a jerk your spouse is? If you cannot tell, I am being facetious and yes, it is to make a point.

Your divorce attorney's primary job is to navigate your legal minefield. They are going to use their time and expertise to advise you on the law, to discuss and prepare case strategy, to review your documents for potential evidence and, if necessary, to go into court to fight your legal battle. It is important to have a good, comfortable working relationship with your attorney. But that is the scope of your relationship—working. Specifically, *she* works for *you*. And believe me, you are paying for it! As I often explain to clients, in a different context you and your attorney could be the best of friends. Besties do not charge for every phone call, text message or email exchanged; divorce lawyers do.

So, as much as your lawyer may like you personally, he calls you with a specific intent. Try to take a clue from him and ensure your communication with him is just as purposeful. This is one way to ensure your retainer deposit isn't used up on phone calls and emails. As one of my colleagues quips, "it is expensive to cry in your attorney's office."

a. That's what friends are for

Divorce can be one of the most emotionally tumultuous times of your life; do not go it alone. Share with family and close friends that are you are going through this process. Organize your support network. Join a support group in your geographic, social or religious community. Solicit a few close friends as your "padded walls" with whom to share your emotions. You may find you lose some personal relationships as friends and family members choose sides. However, you may also gain some unexpected allies: co-workers or neighbors who have experienced divorce.

The positive side of modern divorce rates is that you are not alone. When you have a strong network of support, you will be able to purge your emotional response with them. Then when you meet with your attorney, you are in a better position to focus on the technical aspects of the divorce process.

b. Right professional for the right purpose

Divorce and family law attorneys are usually jacks of all trades and masters of one—that is, the law. A good divorce lawyer will have some knowledge of finance, tax law, retirement and investment benefits, psychological disorders. A *great* lawyer will refer you to the appropriate professional to address non-legal issues.

Need to evaluate the tax consequences of claiming only one of the two children on your income tax return? Talk to a tax professional. Want to know the value of the latest spousal support offer? You need a referral to a certified financial planner. A parenting coordinator can help you and your spouse fashion a child custody schedule and create a process for settling small but regular disputes. Do you need someone to talk to because you are *still* crying in your attorney's office at umpteen dollars per quarter of an hour? Perhaps you should engage a divorce coach or counselor.

Picking the right professional for the right purpose is helpful for so many reasons. You get the benefit of expert advice. You save money, as the professionals I identified above are usually less expensive than your attorney. And the advice and guidance you receive from these professionals can help you and your attorney prepare a strong legal position that will work to your advantage emotionally, financially and legally.

c. "Me" Time

Another way to avoid an expensive divorce is to avoid making your divorce your hobby. I have had clients who meditate on their divorce day and night. They obsess over the details of the break-up, who their spouse is dating, how many ways to get back at the other person, pouring over the financial disclosures like researching a dissertation. I am a strong proponent of clients being engaged and active in the process. As I said above, don't "sleep walk" through your divorce.

However, your divorce should not be your hobby. It should not be your job. Divorce is an experience in your life; it should not *be* your life. It has been my experience that clients for whom the divorce process becomes all consuming, it really consumes all. And the end result is that the attorney makes a lot of money, and the client is lost financially and emotionally.

It is for this reason that I tell clients to "get a hobby." There is a way even the negative experience of divorce can result in some positive developments in your life. Take that language class! Hit the gym! Learn to crochet! Put in some volunteer hours at the community center or the ASPCA. When you start focusing on life beyond the divorce, you will actually see your life beyond the divorce. And you will find that sitting in your attorney's office is an expensive waste of time.

[1] http://www.divorcestatistics.info/how-much-does-divorce-cost-in-the-usa.html

3. Divorce Court is Not Reality T.V.: options beyond going to trial:

Television shows like Divorce Court can give the impression that divorces are tight messy balls that can magically be untangled in 10-15 minutes segments. As most adults (hopefully) understand, however, reality is not reality t.v. Yet in the world of televised 30- minute resolution and a culture of "NOW," many clients are unpleasantly surprise to learn the process of divorce can take one to two years—

occasionally longer if the case is hotly contested. Fighting in court can be very draining, emotionally and financially.

Thankfully, trial is not your only option. There are many alternative dispute resolution options that allow you and your spouse to work out issues of custody, support and division of assets and debt, as opposed to having a judge decide. The more popular of these options include mediation, arbitration and collaborative divorce process.

a. Mediation

Of the three options I have identified, mediation is by far the most well-known, and the most popular. Mediation involves you and your spouse (and, at your option, your attorneys) engaging with a third-party neutral to help facilitate an agreement. Mediators can be retired judges or attorneys, active attorneys, licensed counselors or other non-legal professionals. They are called "neutrals" because they are professionals without a dog in the fight. The goal of a mediator is to help parties reach an agreement.

Regardless of their backgrounds, all certified mediators have gone through an extensive training and a certification process to ensure that they know what they are doing. Training, certification and experience equal effectiveness.

Effectiveness is important. While mediation can be significantly less expensive than trial, most mediators charge a fee. You want to avoid working with an ineffective mediator, because if the mediation is not effective you may end up going to trial anyway! Just like in choosing an attorney, seek recommendations (including from your attorney) for an effective mediator.

Mediation allows you and your spouse to have control over the outcome. Leaving your fate in the hands of a judge is a risky proposition. Despite their best efforts, even good judges can have backgrounds or experience, or just a bad day, which may influence their perspective of you and your case. Mediation means that the people knowledgeable of the circumstances and most affected by the outcome—you and your spouse—determine the outcome.

However, mediation, like the settlement it will hopefully generate, is voluntary. If your spouse is not willing to participate in mediation, no amount of effort to force it will help you, but it may cost you. Even if you can persuade an unwilling spouse to participate in mediation, if they are not participating with an interest in cooperation and compromise, you are wasting time and money. I have more than one experience with clients spending thousands of dollars insisting on mediation with a noncooperative party. In each of the cases I can readily recall, we still went to trial. But not before each client had spent a large amount of money insisting on mediation.

b. Arbitration

Arbitration is another great alternative option. Arbitration in the divorce context is a helpful hybrid of mediation and trial. It involves a third party neutral acting as a judge to make final decisions on one or several issues, or on the entire divorce case. The parties select the arbiter, just as they would a mediator. The parties decide what issues the arbiter will address. Like a trial, each party can present witnesses and evidence, and make arguments. At the end of the arbitration session, the arbiter will make a decision that the parties will likely have agreed in advance is final and binding.

This option gives the parties a lot of flexibility and choice. This means some control over the outcome. However, it also gives the parties finality, just as if they went to court to have a judge decide. However, because you are paying an arbiter to decide the issues you choose at the time you choose, you avoiding the expense of a long, drawn-out divorce process.

c. Collaborative Divorce Process

Compared to the first two alternative resolution options, collaborative divorce process is a new phenomenon that is still gaining recognition and traction. Of the three options, collaborative process requires the greatest level of cooperation. This is where you agree to lay everything on the line. The parties and their attorney pull together a team of professionals to address the contested issues of the case: accountants, child therapists, financial advisors, realtors. A team can consist of whoever the parties and their attorney believe can provide the expertise necessary so that the parties can reach a resolution.

This process saves money by allowing the parties to share the costs of the experts and professionals involved. Remember, the parties can engage as many or as few professionals as they agree are necessary to help them address their issues. There is no costly discovery process—the parties voluntarily disclose any and all documents that are helpful to resolution. Like mediation, the goal of the collaborative process is to help the parties facilitate an agreement.

So far this is all sounding great, right? So, what is the catch? Why isn't everyone engaging in collaborative divorce process?

Here is the rub: a genuine collaborative divorce process also requires the parties and their professionals—including attorneys—to agree that if the process is unsuccessful, the parties will start the divorce process over with *new* professionals. This includes both parties engaging new attorneys! The impetus behind this significant concession is to ensure that both parties come into the process in good faith and with a sincere commitment to cooperative resolution. Collaborative divorce process is a relatively low cost, low conflict alternative to trial, but with significantly higher stakes compared to the first two options. Admittedly, it is not for the faint of heart!

4. *The Heart of the Matter: deemphasizing fault*

Divorce is the result a breakdown in the relationship between married partners. It is usually not caused by a single catastrophic event. Instead, it is a series of little incidents or irritations that build up until one or both parties decide, "I just can't take it anymore!" It's no one's fault or it's everyone's fault. At the end of the day, two people determine they just don't want to be married to each other anymore.

However, there are still many cases that involve one person being caught off guard when his spouse takes some action to unilaterally break up the parties' happy home. Whether it is adultery, abandonment, physical or emotional abuse, sometimes one party is at fault for causing the divorce. Sometimes the parties are in dispute as to who committed the first fault the lead to the end of the marriage. Regardless fault-based divorce is still alive and well in the United States.

Most people are familiar with the common fault-based grounds for divorce—adultery, desertion/abandonment, cruelty. Whether they file for divorce on this basis or not, it has been my experience that most couples assert one of these grounds as the reason for their divorce. These fault grounds are "the heart of the matter," so to speak. It is overwhelmingly emotions that lead people to divorce.

While emotions lead be to divorce, the reality is placing too much emphasis on the emotional aspect of divorce can actually drive up the cost of a divorce. The significance of fault as a basis for divorce has decreased in a society where divorce is frequent and normalized. Emotions in divorce cost a lot and pay very little.

There are many reasons for the changed perspective regarding the importance of fault. The evolving role of women in families and workplace, and their increased financial empowerment is one reason. The nearly eradicated stigma that was historically associated with divorce. The societal trend of divorcing couples just wanting "out" and the response of state legislatures and courts in making it easier for people to do so. Today, all states have some form of "no fault" divorce.

What does this mean in terms of focusing on the things that matter? Three things:

a. Your attorney is a counselor at law—not anything else

You may be starting to notice a pattern here. However, I don't think it can be overemphasized: it is very expensive to treat your attorney as a therapist. It costs money to cry in your attorney's office. Your attorney is not trained to address the emotional episodes you may be experiencing during this process. Your attorney does need to know information about the circumstances and breakdown of the marriage to formulate strategy. However, she does not need to be reminded your spouse is a homewrecker every time you talk to her. I advise most of my clients to seek the assistance of a therapist or, at a minimum, a divorce coach. Talk to your attorney about what she knows best: the law. Which leads me to my next point.

b. Listen to the advice you paid your attorney for

So, you may not be the one treating your attorney like a marriage counselor. Perhaps instead you are just not listening to him at all. I don't care how many times you have been married. As a professional family law attorney I promise I have experienced more divorces than you. Or this may be your first divorce. If you have followed the advice I provided earlier in the chapter, it won't be your attorney's first. That is why it is important to listen to your attorney's advice, which is based on his or her experience.

Your attorney is assessing the facts and circumstances of your case. They are considering the trend or history of the judges sitting in the court in which your case will be heard. They are probably familiar with the reputation and tactics of your opposing counsel. He or she is going to talk to you about whether you should pay the private investigator the follow your spouse, and what kind of difference such evidence would make in your case. Or, that it won't make a difference.

Ultimately the decision about whether and how much to emphasize fault in the breakdown of the marriage. I will tell you, however, that I have experienced clients ignore my advice and insist on a course of action that may have gained the moral high ground, but little else. The judge may have granted a divorce on fault grounds, but each party still only received 50% of the marital assets.

This is not to say that fault is never important or that it won't have an impact on divorce proceedings. What I am urging is that you seriously consider your attorney's advice about strategy, method, or whether to pursue a matter at all. You are paying him to do this. Which leads to my final point.

c. Conduct a cost benefit analysis

As with any business or market transaction (because at some levels, a divorce is a business transaction), you should weigh the cost against the benefit you expect to receive. Most attorneys would agree: it very expensive to try a fault-based divorce trial. At the end of the day (or in some cases, two or three days), will it get you what you want? That is an important discussion for you and your attorney. There are certainly scenarios where a fault-based claim may result in recovery of a significant sum of money or asset. Perhaps a fault-based claim positions you to better bargain for increased spousal support or a greater division of retirement assets. But the cost of principle may not equate to the value of your 2007 Honda Accord. Take the fees you would otherwise pay your attorney for principle and buy a new car for your new life!

Your Next, Better Chapter is What Matters

Whether you initiated the divorce, it was forced upon you, or you and your spouse came to a mutual agreement, one thing is certain: divorce is not easy. In fact, divorce is very difficult. That's true whether the decision came suddenly or was firm in someone's mind for years.

Regardless of how or why it came, determine now not to be a victim. Don't let divorce happen to you; instead let it be something you get through. It can be hell. But as Winston Churchill is believed to have said, "if you are going through hell, keep going!" You will get through, you will get beyond, and your future can be better and more than this period.

How do you do this? By focusing on the things that matter. It will be so easy during this time of transition to get sidetracked and distracted by issues that will eventually be part of your past. I want to urge you not to stay there.

Focus instead on the picture of your life when this process is over: what do you want it to look like? How do you want it to feel? How do you want your children to feel? Then translate that into what it will look like in terms of income and asset distribution, time with your children, what property you must have, and what you can live without. This picture is what you take to your attorney. That is what you want her to do for you, and that is the price you are willing to pay—the cost of that next, better chapter.

STEPHANIE L. TANG

Family Law Attorney & Mediator
Kogut & Wilson, L.L.C.

Email: Stephanie@kogutwilson.com

Website: www.kogutwilson.com/attorney-profiles

LinkedIn: www.linkedin.com/in/stephanie-tang

Call: (312) 565-4100

Stephanie L. Tang is a family law attorney, mediator, and collaborative law professional at Kogut & Wilson, L.L.C. She strives to provide personalized attention to her clients by walking them through each step of the litigation or settlement process.

Her effective communication and organizational skills help clients feel comfortable and prepared throughout their case. As a certified mediator and Fellow with the Collaborative Law Institute of Illinois, Stephanie offers clients alternative means to resolve their divorce outside of the courtroom.

Stephanie was previously selected to receive the Avvo Clients' Choice Award in Divorce for outstanding client reviews from clients she represented through divorce proceedings. In support of this award, clients described Stephanie as a "professional, patient, hard worker", "excellent communicator", and an attorney who helped clients "feel calm and prepared in court because of her in-depth preparation."

Stephanie graduated from University of Illinois College of Law, *Magna Cum Laude* with pro bono notation. While in school, Stephanie received CALI Excellence for the Future Awards in Family Law and Regulations of Financial Institutions. Stephanie also received the Marguerite L.

Rickert Award for Excellence in both Legal Writing and Service as one of the top eight students in her graduating class in both areas.

When not helping clients in her private practice, Stephanie is actively involved in pro bono work in the Chicagoland community. In 2017, Stephanie was selected among over 2,300 volunteer attorneys to receive the Distinguished Service Award for outstanding pro bono service by Chicago Volunteer Legal Services, Chicago's first and pre-eminent legal aid organization.

PUTTING TOGETHER THE
PIECES OF THE DIVORCE PUZZLE

By Stephanie L. Tang

For many people, the concept of a "stress-free divorce" may sound like an oxymoron. While it is true that divorce will inevitably lead to stress, there are several steps you may take to alleviate the pressures of divorce and help you feel prepared during an otherwise uncertain time. Think of a divorce case as a large puzzle you need to assemble to see the final picture. You must be equipped with the necessary tips and tools to help you put those pieces together.

Back to the Basics: The Divorce Process in a Nutshell

If someone has a fear of roller coasters, it often helps to look at the coaster's path to understand the dips and turns they will face on the ride. You can apply the same thought process to divorce. It is helpful for people considering divorce to know what the process in court looks like prior to starting it, so they may understand the possible hiccups along the way.

First, if you are the filing party (also known as the "petitioner"), you will need to file a divorce petition. The petition contains basic information about both parties (name, age, employment status), date and place of marriage, any children born to the parties, grounds for divorce, and any requests you have regarding support, property division, and custody issues.

This petition will not only initiate your divorce case, but it can also set the tone for the case moving forward. For example, in Illinois and many other states, a spouse may choose to formally serve the other spouse with the petition or, if they believe their spouse will follow all necessary procedures in a timely manner, may choose to simply give them a copy of the petition.

As you may imagine, many spouses do not take kindly to being formally served by a stranger and at times, are led to become angry and resort to making rash decisions. This can create tension between the parties right from the onset of a divorce. The filing party should therefore think carefully about both where and when to serve their spouse with the petition should they choose this route.

When a spouse is served with the Petition, they will also receive a "Summons," which notifies the spouse of the time period they have to respond to the petition (typically thirty days). If the spouse does not file a Response within the time period allowed, a court may still move forward with the case and enter a final divorce judgment. This judgment will be based primarily on the results the petitioner initially requested in their Petition without any input from their spouse.

This is known as a "default divorce." Once a default divorce judgment is entered, the spouse will have a short period of time to try to motion to court to "vacate" the judgment. If the spouse still fails to file a motion within this time period, the grounds for trying to vacate the judgment become very limited and it becomes much more difficult to try to vacate the judgment.

On the other hand, if your spouse does respond within the time period provided on the Summons, you will then exchange financial disclosure statements outlining your income, assets, and liabilities. These disclosures help your attorneys create balance sheets to negotiate a final settlement of spousal and child support and division of all assets and liabilities.

The final piece of the puzzle is negotiating a final parenting agreement that governs all issues related to making decisions and allocation of parenting time for the children. From initiation through completion of the divorce, there are many considerations people should keep in mind and tips they should follow to ensure divorce stays as "stress free" as possible.

Tips for Negotiating a Financial Settlement

The next piece of the puzzle for people after filing an initial petition is working towards negotiating a financial settlement of the parties' assets and liabilities, child support, and maintenance (otherwise known as alimony).

Tip 1: Understand Your Assets and Liabilities

One of the most common mistakes I see is when one spouse rushes to file for divorce without having an accurate picture of their finances. This is particularly detrimental in cases where one spouse historically handled all of the couple's finances during their marriage and the other spouse is completely in the dark. In such cases, I often find that a spouse who impulsively files for divorce without knowing anything about their spouse's income or assets is placed at a disadvantage when it comes to negotiating a financial settlement.

Accordingly, if you are contemplating filing for divorce or you believe your spouse may soon file for divorce, you should copy and scan all important financial documents including your previous tax returns, statements for all accounts (including credit card, checking, savings, and retirement accounts), and documents related to your and your spouse's income (including pay stubs, W2s, and K1s). This will help you understand what money you have available now and in the future, and what debts you have to pay off. Having this information will in turn help your attorney create a balance sheet of all of your assets and discuss different scenarios for dividing your assets and debts.

Additionally, if your spouse has a history of liquidating or otherwise disposing of assets without your knowledge or consent, you may want to consider talking to your attorney about the possibility of asking the court to enter a temporary restraining order to prevent certain transfers of assets during the pendency of your divorce proceeding. By first understanding and making a list of what accounts you have, you will be able to build a stronger case to present to the judge a potential basis for a restraining order.

Tip 2: Don't Settle Because You're Exhausted

Divorce is a marathon, not a sprint. That being said, divorce can be an emotionally draining process and unfortunately, I often find that clients try to rush into settlements to end the process as fast as possible. Mental exhaustion or frustration often leads clients to neglect their due diligence and enter agreements without carefully contemplating their potential consequences. I constantly advise clients to remember the long-term impact of their divorce and the importance of having financial security following a divorce.

There are two common mistakes I often see when people rush into financial settlement agreements they do not feel comfortable with due to exhaustion or frustration. The first is when one spouse does not take the time to value a marital asset despite believing it is worth more than their spouse has disclosed. This is most common when one spouse owns a business, real estate, or asset of undetermined value and lowballs the value, knowing their spouse wants to get the divorce done and hoping they will not challenge the value.

However, the non-owner spouse may later find out the asset was actually worth much more and they took a lesser value just so they could finish the agreement. At that point, particularly if the spouse did not exercise their due diligence and exhaust available avenues for discovery, it will be difficult for them to ask the family court to vacate the agreement.

A second common mistake occurs when a spouse agrees to sign an agreement to divide assets based on a spouse's initial disclosure despite believing the spouse is hiding assets.

Unfortunately, people lie (whether done on purpose or accidentally), on their financial disclosure statements and fail to disclose certain assets. Sometimes this is done maliciously, where one spouse hopes that the other spouse does not remember he or she has a certain asset and does not want to divide it as part of the final agreement. Sometimes a spouse simply forgets that they have the asset at all. If you remember seeing statements for accounts that are not disclosed on your spouse's financial disclosure, or you remember conversations your spouse had about a certain account, it is a best practice to tell your lawyer about this account, so you both can do your due diligence in confirming this account was closed, or seeing if it still has a balance. If you know your spouse has an account they are not disclosing, you have the option of issuing a Subpoena to the company where the asset is held and asking for all statements associated with the asset/account.

Tip 3: It's Just a Sofa

I often see cases where people get emotionally attached to particular items of personal property in a divorce and their attachment stalls the entire settlement process. In one case I handled, the parties were able to settle all matters except who would be awarded the parties' designer sofa. The parties had bought the sofa together and they both refused to let the other party have it. After numerous letters between myself and the opposing attorney and angry texts between the parties, the Judge ultimately told the parties to flip a coin to decide who got it.

In these cases, it is better for parties to try to negotiate on their own if they can and if not, they should keep in mind that most items are replaceable and it is likely for the best to start anew with brand new furniture and items after their divorce is finalized. This not only gives you a fresh start following a divorce, but it can help save hundreds (or even thousands) of dollars in attorneys' fees and hours of your time and allow you to focus on your assets as a whole.

In the same vein, you should remember to look at the big picture when negotiating a financial settlement, rather than focusing on individual items such as a sofa. By looking at division of assets one at a time, you do not see how the whole division, timing and taxes are coming together for your final settlement. Furthermore, by letting emotions lead your negotiations, you may also forego a better settlement offer because you are fixated on retaining your favorite car or your entire 401(k) account balance.

Tip 4: Consider the Impact of Taxes

At times, people make the mistake of not considering the tax consequences of their divorce settlement and the potential impact of child and spousal support received. The best way to understand the true impact of a deal is to look at the value of all assets and support each spouse receives on an after-tax basis. Generally, spousal support payments are deductible by a payor spouse and taxable to the payee spouse. In contrast, child support is not taxable or deductible to either spouse.

Additionally, some assets, including certain retirement accounts (e.g. IRAs) or capital gains, are tax-deferred, which means any interest is tax free until the spouse takes constructive receipt of the interest. The best idea is to discuss potential tax consequences of any settlement proposal with your attorney and accountant to determine the fairness of a deal before agreeing to it.

Tip 5: Consider Reasons for Deviation When Calculating Support

States employ different models when calculating spousal and child support. For example, the majority of states have adopted the "income shares" model for child support (looking at both parents' income in calculating support), but a minority still use the "percentage of income" model (looking only at the percentage of one spouse's income). Regardless of the model they use, there are often "guideline" support amounts derived from applying the applicable model. People often accept these guideline amounts as fact, but most state statutes provide "deviation factors" that would justify deviating from these amounts. For example, a deviating factor for spousal support may be if the payor spouse agrees to pay other household expenses (such as a mortgage) for the residence where the payee spouse lives for a certain period of time instead and their spousal support obligation is reduced accordingly.

In Illinois, deviation factors for child support may include where the parents have to pay extraordinary medical expenditures necessary to preserve the life or health of one parent or their child or the parents have to pay additional expenses because their child has extraordinary medical, physical, or developmental needs. If factors such as these exist in your case, it is helpful to look at potential deviation from guidelines.

There may also be reasons for deviating from a spouse's actual income when calculating guideline support. In Illinois and many other states, a spouse's income may be "imputed" to a higher income if the court finds he or she is voluntarily unemployed or underemployed, unreasonably failed to take advantage of an employment opportunity, or is intentionally trying to avoid their support obligation. When deciding what income to impute, courts will look to factors including a spouse's employment potential, prior work history, occupational qualifications, prevailing job opportunities, and earning levels in the community. If a court ultimately decides deviating from guidelines or imputing income is appropriate, it could make a big difference in the amount of support a spouse is ordered to pay.

Tip 6: Provide and Enforce Timelines for Transfers of Assets or Title

Another common mistake parties make is not providing for or enforcing a timeline for division and transfer of assets. I have read many agreements that state a party is responsible for payment of half of all of the child's extracurricular activity expenses but do not provide any timeline of when this money needs to be transferred to the receiving spouse. Alternatively, I have read agreements where one party is ordered to refinance the mortgage on the marital residence and remove their spouse's name from the title, but again, they provide no timeline for when this refinance must occur. This leads to ambiguity and fights between parties over when the money must be paid or title must be transferred. At times, the party receiving a benefit is forced back into court with a weak argument to enforce or clarify the agreement because no timeline was initially set.

Along the same lines, I have also seen cases where parties believe the assets awarded to them in a final settlement agreement are magically transferred to them upon entry of their divorce Judgment. This is often not the case. For example, division of certain retirement accounts including pensions and employer-sponsored retirement plans requires entry of a separate order known as a Qualified Domestic Relations Order (QDRO). If a QDRO is not entered, the former spouse will have no rights to the participant spouse's retirement benefits. This hypothetical highlights the importance of not only putting in timelines for transfers of assets, but also diligently following up on these timelines to ensure they are followed.

Tips for Negotiating a Final Parenting Agreement

The other major piece of the puzzle that requires careful negotiation is all issues related to any minor children of the parties. In Illinois and several other states, the concept of "custody" has been replaced by a new term: "allocation of parental responsibilities" ("APR"). APR is further divided into two categories: allocation of significant decision-making responsibilities (related to the children's education, health, religion, and extracurricular activities) and allocation of parenting time. Similarly, the majority of states still use the term "custody," which is further divided into "legal custody" (determining which parent can make significant legal decisions for the child) and "physical custody" (determining which parent, if any, has a majority of parenting time). Regardless of the nomenclature, negotiating final parenting agreements can be a particularly thorny and emotional rollercoaster for both parents. That being said, there are steps parents should take to help ensure a smooth transition from a one to a two-household family.

Tip 1: *Think About What is in the Best Interests of Your Children*

All states and the District of Columbia have adopted statutes that require family courts to consider the "best interests" of the children when making decisions related to APR/custody. While there is no standardized definition of "best interests," several state statutes list specific factors that courts should consider, which commonly include, but are not limited to:

- Any mental or physical health needs of the children

- Any mental or physical health needs of the parents

- The emotional relationship between the children and their parents, siblings, and other household members (such as relatives or significant others)

- The ability for each parent to provide a safe and stable environment for the children, including provision of necessities including food, clothing, and medical care. In considering this factor, courts often also look to the employment schedule for each parent (night shifts, flexibility, unpredictable hours) in terms of its impact on a parent's ability to exercise regular and consistent parenting time

- Any incidents of domestic violence in the home

Unfortunately, in many cases, spouses sometimes harbor a great deal of anger and hurt towards the other spouse and use parenting negotiations as a means to spite the other person. In other cases, parents fight the entry of parenting schedules because they do not want to pay child support. Regardless, when parents put their needs first, it is ultimately detrimental to the children caught in the middle and causes unnecessary delays in litigation.

This advice extends beyond negotiating the terms of the agreement itself to governing the behavior of parents during the negotiation process. Specifically, parents should not put their children between them by asking them to pick sides during the divorce. In fact, many states have custody statutes that direct courts to consider whether one parent has "alienated" a child from the other parent through their unilateral actions. Courts often find alienation has occurred where one parent either insults or vilifies the other parent to the child on a constant basis. If a court finds one parent has tried to alienate the children from the other parent, that factor will swing heavily in favor of the other parent. Accordingly, parents need to resist the urge to blame each other for any bumps down the road in front of the children.

Tip 2: Walk Through the Proposed Parenting Schedule

Generally, the most helpful tool for my clients is going through a hypothetical year with them as if the agreement was already entered. We first go through what a regular week will look like, including who will be transporting the children to and from parenting time and at what times these drop-offs and pick-ups will occur. This helps clients envision what their everyday life will look like and whether the schedule outlined in their draft agreement is one they can see themselves following moving forward.

An example of a realization that comes from this exercise is illustrated in cases where parents do not want their spouses coming to their house following a divorce because they would rather that remain their separate space. In these cases, clients often realize after thinking about the proposed schedule that they do not want pick-ups and drop-offs of the children to occur at their house. Instead, they pick a neutral, and often happier, location for the children such as a nearby ice cream shop or library for the exchange.

We then go through the school breaks- spring break, winter break, and summer vacation. Many parents want to take their children on trips during these times and it is important to make sure each parent can take their vacation time and enjoy extended time with their children. However, the other parent should still be entitled to an itemized itinerary and video and/or phone time with the children.

Finally, we go through the holiday schedule to ensure all the major holidays are covered. When I say "major holidays", it is important to note that it's up to the parents to let their lawyers know if a holiday holds certain meaning to them, whether it has a religious significance or if the holiday is accompanied by a specific holiday tradition.

For example, I had a client specifically request that they were awarded Labor Day weekend every year because they had an annual family tradition of flying to Colorado for a family reunion. I had another client request that she got to spend time with the children on Day of the Dead every year so she could teach the children about the culture and tradition behind the holiday. This knowledge helps lawyers customize agreements so they fit with the needs and interests of the family moving forward.

Tip 3: Do Not Sign an Agreement You Do Not Understand or Are Not Comfortable With

One common mistake in negotiating custody agreements is rushing to enter an incomplete agreement that you do not fully understand and are not fully comfortable with. Divorce can be a very emotional process and I have read parenting agreements that were entered with the court by parents who were following the philosophy that something was better than nothing.

However, this often results in agreements that do not encompass the details that should be included in a custody agreement such as a holiday or vacation schedule or aspects related to making major decisions for a child. Thus, I see many cases where parties are coming back into court to fight because of big gaps they failed to address in their initial custody negotiations. This costs parties more legal fees on the back-end and often wastes more time and causes more frustration than if they had addressed these issues in the initial agreement.

Tip 4: "Cookie Cutter" Parenting Agreements Do Not Exist

Parents often hope to simplify the negotiation process by entering into a "cookie cutter" parenting agreement that vaguely touches upon issues relating to their children. However, parents need to understand and embrace that each child and each family is different and parenting agreements should reflect that uniqueness.

As a more unusual example, I worked on one case where the parents asked me to draft a parenting schedule taking into account pick-up and drop-off their child's giant stuffed animal. In this case, the child needed this particular stuffed animal to sleep at night but was not permitted to bring it to school. I ended up writing a separate schedule for the parents to coordinate dropping off the stuffed animal so the child would have the stuffed animal every night despite sleeping in different homes.

A more common scenario I have encountered is when the children need specific medications during parenting time. In one case I handled, the child of the parties had life-threatening allergies to peanuts and milk. The parents, opposing attorney, and I worked together to draft language that provided both parents would always have EpiPens on hand during parenting time, would try to keep them at room temperature, and would be responsible for purchasing replacement EpiPens if they lost them.

Tip 5: Try to be Flexible

No matter how hard you try to plan for it, divorce is a difficult adjustment, particularly when parents have young children who are transitioning from living in one household to two. I have received numerous calls and emails from clients who want to file a petition against their spouse for being five minutes late to dropping the kids off. I have also received calls and emails from clients wanting to file a petition against their spouse because they refused to take their child to sports practice when it was scheduled during their parenting time. Parents need to be willing to exercise a certain amount of flexibility to accommodate their children's schedules and to a given extent, their ex-spouse's schedule.

To help address this issue, many parents choose to add a "good faith flexibility" clause into their parenting agreements that provide parents should be flexible in accommodating each other's obligations that necessitate a change in parenting time. This clause also typically provides that the parties acknowledge that it is in the best interests of the children to attend "unusual events" including weddings, funerals, and other one-time events that cannot be rescheduled, as well as their regularly scheduled extracurricular activities and practices.

Finally, this clause commonly states that parents should provide each other with as much advance notice as possible if they are not going to be able to exercise their parenting time as scheduled. Going through the exercise of writing and reviewing this language often helps parents remember the importance of prioritizing their children's needs over their feelings towards their spouse.

Understanding the Alternatives to Litigation

Contrary to popular belief, there are a couple of alternatives to traditional in-court litigation for a divorce. By understanding these alternatives, spouses can feel more confident in their choice of procedure and what each process will entail.

Mediation

Mediation is a process in which a neutral third party (the mediator) helps parties reach a mutual resolution of issues in their divorce case. A mediator is not there to take the side of one party over the other. Instead, the mediator will help parties try to reach a solution that satisfies their respective needs and interests. Mediation is completely voluntary and confidential so if one spouse decides mediation is no longer productive, they can stop the process knowing that nothing they propose in mediation can be used against them in a court proceeding. Mediation can be limited in scope to certain issues (such as parenting time) or you could choose to mediate your whole case to try to come to a comprehensive agreement.

Many couples like mediation because it gives couples the flexibility to make their own decisions that they believe work best for their family rather than leaving it to a Judge who may not understand all the nuances of their marriage and family. However, mediation likely will not work when one or both spouses are hiding assets or income or if one or both spouses refuse to engage in a good faith effort at approaching a settlement.

Collaborative Divorce

Collaborative divorce is an alternative to litigation that is gaining substantial traction in the United States. In a collaborative divorce, each parent has their own attorney, but they also hire other professionals including child specialists, financial advisors (often CDFAs), and coaches as well. The professionals and the parties work together as a team in out-of-court meetings to address outstanding issues and reach a full and final settlement that will meet the parties' respective needs and interests. Once a settlement is reached outside of court, the attorneys will prepare documents memorializing the agreement for filing with the court.

If you follow the collaborative approach, you and your spouse will first each sign a Participation Agreement. This Agreement provides that you and your spouse will engage in a good faith efforts to settle the case, exchange complete financial information, and maintain absolute confidentiality. Confidentiality in this context means you cannot later use any settlement offers used during the collaborative process if your case ultimately does not settle.

There are three major benefits to a collaborative divorce compared to litigation: better control, more privacy, and less adversity between parties. First, parties feel they have better control over the process because they set the timing and agenda for each team meeting. Second, unlike "traditional" divorces where parties appear in court on multiple occasions and expose their issues to the public, collaborative divorce is kept out of court until the final agreement is set.

Finally, by agreeing to a collaborative divorce, the parties and their attorneys agree to mutually respect each other and be transparent with each other. Therefore, attorneys will not have an incentive to drag the process out longer. Like in mediation, collaborative divorce likely may not be a good fit if one spouse believes the other spouse is intentionally hiding assets.

When Should I File For Divorce?

Timing is an important consideration for parties contemplating divorce for several reasons, both emotional and financial. On the emotional end, January is often a popular time for people to file because it is right after the big block of winter holidays but before Valentine's Day. The idea is to wait until after the holidays, especially for couples with children, so that the children can still have a happy time during the holidays and there is no added stress to the already hectic holiday season. Parties with teenage children may decide to wait to file for divorce until after their children graduate from high school so as not to cause tension at home while their children are applying for college and generally busy being a teenager.

There are also considerations on the legal side that parties should consider. For example, in Illinois, the duration of maintenance (previously known as alimony) a spouse is entitled to receive may increase significantly depending on how many years you are married. Specifically, the law provides the duration of maintenance shall be calculated by multiplying the length of the marriage on the date of filing by one of the following multipliers: 5 years or less: 0.2; more than 5 years and less than 10 years: 0.4; 10 years or more but less than 15 years: 0.6; 15 years or more but less than 20 years: 0.8; 20 or more years: either permanent maintenance or equal to duration of marriage.

This means if a couple is married for five years, the lower-income-earning spouse may only be entitled to one year of maintenance. However, if a couple is married for five years and one month, the lower-income-earning spouse may be entitled to over two years of maintenance. This example highlights the difference waiting one month could make if you wait or rush to file.

Steps to Take After Your Divorce is Finalized

The tips as outlined above will help you navigate the tricky negotiations associated with divorce. However, even once the divorce is finalized, there are still steps every person should take to finish the puzzle:

Step 1: Develop a New Monthly Budget

Common sense dictates that it is more expensive to maintain two households compared to one. However, many people do not realize the reality of that statement until after their divorce is finalized. It is a good idea to sit down with your attorney or financial planner to create a snapshot of what assets you received pursuant to your final divorce and what amounts, if any, you will start paying to or receiving from your ex-spouse on a monthly basis.

This snapshot should also include any liabilities you are now responsible for paying, including mortgage payments, real estate taxes, and any car loans. From there, you can work on setting new spending goals, managing your expectations for monthly expenses, and creating a plan moving forward for investment and allocation of your assets and liabilities.

Step 2: Update Your Estate Planning Documents and Powers of Attorney

After a divorce, people frequently forget to update their estate planning documents (e.g. wills, powers of attorney) and beneficiaries to their accounts (e.g. IRAs, life insurance policies). This would mean that if the person died after the divorce without changing these documents, the estate that they would otherwise pass to their children or other relatives would instead pass entirely to their ex-spouse. Once your divorce is finalized, you should make sure to update these types of documents to ensure your updated desires are accurately reflected.

Step 3: Follow Up on Derivative Benefits

When a couple is married for at least ten years, the unemployed or lower-earning spouse is often entitled to receive social security benefits even after a divorce. Specifically, an ex-spouse will be eligible to receive these benefits if: they are unmarried and at least 62 years old, their ex is entitled to Social Security retirement benefits, and the benefits they would be entitled to pursuant to their own record are less than the benefits they would receive on their ex-spouse's record. Even if your ex-spouse has not applied for benefits but is at least 62 and qualifies to receive the benefits, you could still receive benefits through his record if you meet these requirements and you have been divorced for at least two years.

Step 4: Follow and Enforce Provisions of the Final Agreements

People often mistakenly believe that just because an agreement is entered means the other spouse will follow the provisions. Unfortunately, there are many cases where a spouse decides not to uphold their obligations under the final agreements, whether it is by failing to transfer title to an asset or failure to pay spousal or child support.

In these instances, it is often advisable for the parties to go back to court to enforce the obligation sooner rather than later. Otherwise, if a person waits too long to bring a claim in court, a judge may find too much time has passed and your claim is barred for being brought too late or you may lose key documentation you need to prove your ex-spouse is not complying with court orders.

Putting the Puzzle Pieces Together

People often view divorce as one of the most emotional times of their lives. However, there are steps people can take to minimize stress and prepare for negotiations when moving forward with divorce. Following the tips as outlined above will provide you with the tools you need to finish the puzzle and finalize your "stress-free" divorce.

Stephanie L. Tang is a family law attorney, mediator, & collaborative law professional at Kogut & Wilson, L.L.C. Stephanie's practice is in Chicago, Illinois and she handles divorce and parentage matters in Cook and all surrounding counties. She can be reached at (312) 565-4100 or by e-mail at Stephanie@KogutWilson.com.

Her website is http://www.KogutWilson.com. Contact her for a free hour-long consultation today!

MARY SALISBURY (CDFA)

Certified Divorce Financial Analyst

The Right Divorce Solution, LLC

Email: mary@TheRightDivorceSolution.com

Website: www.TheRightDivorceSolution.com

LinkedIn: www.linkedin.com/in/maryhsalisbury

Call: (910) 622-7180

During her career as an Independent Financial Advisor, Mary obtained the designation of Certified Divorce Financial Analyst. Mary developed a passion for helping individuals and couples have a better divorce experience, so much so, that she sold her advisory book of business so she could focus solely on this aspect of her profession.

Mary graduated from the University of Miami with a degree in economics then spent 11 years as an employee benefits and retirement plan (ERISA) paralegal. She obtained the designations of Certified Pension Consultant and Qualified Pension Administrator. That in-depth knowledge of retirement plans, IRAs and employee benefits adds to her expertise as a Certified Divorce Financial Analyst®.

Mary has also acquired in-depth knowledge of the complex rules regarding Social Security which helps her guide her clients close to retirement, navigate the complex rules governing this critical source of retirement income. Mary retained her life and health insurance licenses so she could help protect child and spousal support for her divorcing clients.

When not helping clients in Wilmington, NC and the surrounding areas, you can find Mary playing competitive and recreational tennis or spending time with friends, family and her dog. Mary volunteers for a local animal rescue organization and uses her handyman skills as a volunteer at Habitat for Humanity projects.

THE RIGHT DIVORCE SOLUTION
By Mary Salisbury

Stress free divorce? Is there such a thing? I think not, but I think the choices one makes when thinking about divorce, going through divorce and post-divorce can make a huge difference in how well you go through the divorce process, both emotionally and financially. I believe the choices made when entering the divorce process are the most significant, and will have the biggest effect on the emotional and financial stress you go through.

Most people think they have two choices when it comes to divorce: either get an attorney or go through a divorce on their own. Couples who have significant assets or who have been married for a significant period of time think that they <u>have</u> to hire an attorney to divide up their assets. That simply is not true.

Although I am often hired to be the financial advocate for just one of the parties in a divorce, I prefer to facilitate settlements between divorcing couples in a financially guided manner without the added cost of including attorneys in that process. Legal bills are one of the biggest stressors and sources of animosity in divorce and using my services as a financial neutral allows couples to divorce much more affordably. Once they agree upon a settlement, I then send the couple to attorneys for preparation of the legal paperwork.

This entire process often costs less than what ONE attorney in my geographic area commonly charges as a retainer. When I talk to the public about my beliefs and my alternative solution, the most frequent response I hear is "Where were you when I divorced [X number of] years ago?" Most people have no idea this solution exists.

I was married for 26 years before I divorced. I was fortunate to have a financial and legal background and I was responsible for the household bills and investments. Even so, it was the scariest time of my life. Going from comfortable in retirement to "Oh no, now I have half and where will that leave me?" is bad enough. Then there is the emotional loss of someone who was your best friend for years. Believe me, I can relate to what my clients are going through. I wanted to create a business to help people get through a difficult situation with less stress.

I find many of my clients have a respect for the love they once had, although it's gone, and that is why they choose my process. They realize that through social ties and family, and especially if they had children together, their ex will continue to be a part of their life. They know the future holds weddings, grandchildren and family gatherings. They want to take the stress off their children; children deserve better.

I'm inspired by stories I hear from people who decided to forego the attorney route and negotiated their divorce settlement. They tell me how years later they can get along with their ex. They might not be friends (although some are), but they can be at family gatherings where no one feels particularly uncomfortable. Many acknowledge they could have fought for more, but they got on with their lives and they and their families are the better for it. Having a kinder divorce especially appeals to those with strong Christian values. One Pastor I explained my services to even went so far as to say I had a ministry. I took that as a great compliment.

Some people say there is no such thing as an amicable divorce. Maybe that's true because Merriam-Webster defines amicable as "characterized by friendly goodwill: peaceable". Most divorcing couples aren't feeling very friendly, in the best of cases. But that doesn't mean everyone wants to duke it out with attorneys. Many are just done, and they want it over. They need guidance on division of property and support issues but most cannot afford and/or don't want to pay the average $15,000 it costs to hire attorneys for a divorce in the U.S. today.

How can hiring a CDFA reduce stress in my divorce?

The emotional aspect of divorce, particularly when one spouse feels they are not at fault, can leave that spouse believing that he or she is entitled to a certain amount of money as part of a divorce settlement, even if it's not what's available, what they need, or what they are entitled to. Many have false expectations that they will be able to secure a divorce settlement allowing them to continue with their accustomed style of living. Or the opposite may be true; one spouse may think they are being taken to the cleaners when actually their long term cash flow and net worth will be just fine. When you know how much money you and your spouse have and what you will need to meet your basic expenses, and what your future cash flow and net worth look like, it's easier to reach a compromise in a divorce. **Compromising (settling) your divorce quickly, but in a financially educated manner, will save thousands, and both parties can get on with their lives.**

Although Certified Divorce Financial Analysts (CDFAs) have been around for about 20 years, there are not enough of us in full-fledged divorce practice so individuals, and even most family law attorneys, don't know what we do or the advantages of using us. If you are reading this book, you are fortunate, because you will discover the true benefits of hiring a CDFA.

The advantages of financial guidance during a divorce

When you think about it, a divorce is mainly a financial settlement. The biggest misconception that people have when they hire an attorney is that their attorney will give them the financial guidance they need. Attorneys are professionals trained to advise and protect people's legal rights, and they must have a depth of knowledge in all areas of the law in which they practice in order to represent their clients adequately. It is not fair or reasonable to expect that they will also have the depth of knowledge that a CDFA has about taxes, pension distributions, insurance issues, long-term ramifications of property division or financial planning.

To obtain the CDFA designation, the professional must have a financial or divorce background. Many CDFAs are accountants, financial advisors and mediators. The curriculum of study includes:

- an overview of divorce procedures and laws

- a study of the in-depth financial aspects of divorce including

- how to define and categorize property

- how to determine the value of retirement plans

- how to recognize options for the marital home

- understand the fundamentals of alimony and child support and

- how divorce affects Social Security benefits

- a study of the tax issues of divorce including

  - the complex tax issues of dividing property

  - selling the marital home

  - transferring retirement benefits

  - giving and receiving support

  - potential changes on a personal income tax return as someone goes from "Married Filing Jointly" to "Single" or "Head of Household."

Who benefits from using a CDFA?

Typical divorcing clients have assets such as a home, rental properties, a pension or a 401(k), IRAs and/or stock and bonds. They also have debts such as their mortgage, credit cards and student loans. Often my clients have been married at least fifteen years and sometimes over 25 years. Divorce in long term marriages ("grey divorce") is a growing trend and there is a lot of complexity in dividing everything up. Many people, even those with high net worth, are lost when it comes to splitting their finances. One or both may not know what their assets are really worth.

No matter how you cut it, when two households, rather than one, are operating on the same amount of money, everyone is worse off. There is a tremendous amount of worry associated with how expenses will be covered.

I'm often told by people I meet that they thought they had to hire an attorney because they have children, and they didn't know how to deal with child custody and child support issues. In many states, including North Carolina where I reside, child support is determined by guidelines. People don't realize "there's an app for that". Why pay an attorney to calculate payments you can calculate yourself? These guidelines are followed in most cases, unless it can be shown that they are unjust or inappropriate.

In my state, child support is based on overnight stays, so unfortunately people get caught in court battles fighting for more custody to get more child support. Unscrupulous attorneys use this as a vehicle for billing more hours. A couple easily can spend $10,000 fighting over child custody to get $200 more per month. That's 50 months of child support that went to attorneys rather than their children.

There are those cases, such as abuse and drug or alcohol addiction, where one parent should not have custody, and in those cases, the parent seeking custody needs the power of the court. But barring such a reason, if a couple cannot agree on child custody, they should see a family therapist or a pastor to get that resolved. Health insurance often covers therapy and pastors are free. Child psychologists can guide the couple and educate them on their child's parental and emotional development needs, and help parents attend to the needs of their child first. Once child custody is resolved, I can use the guidelines that are programed in my software to help you determine child support.

The analysis procedure

With the exception of child custody, divorce is about money; division of property and debt and determining the amount of support. When I am hired to work with a couple as a financial neutral and first meet them, I will talk with each individual separately so I can learn about their role in the relationship, their work history and earning capacity, and their post-divorce goals. I ask them to gather and provide me their financial documents and budgets. That data is put into specialized family law software and from there I start my analysis.

It's not just the financial software that's the benefit, it's my financial expertise and experience in financial planning that drives the way the financial software is used that is so beneficial. While analyzing my client's financial information and inputting the data in the software, I'm thinking about questions such as: Is their monthly budget realistic and how will their near term plans affect their budget over the next few years? Have they thought about expenses such as life insurance and health insurance? Do they believe their income will increase and by how much?

Generally, when it comes to dividing assets and debts, states are either community property (a 50/50 split of marital assets) or equitable division (where the starting point is 50/50 and you negotiate from there to determine an "equitable" division). What is equitable is based on varying criteria in each state, but they all boil down to money.

A CDFA understands how financial drivers such as tax laws, capital gains and inflation affect the sale and transfer of assets. Using my financial expertise, I can structure settlements to save money in a variety of ways. For instance, often I am able to structure a settlement in more tax-efficient ways, saving money. I can make sure the agreement to split any pension plans is worded to assure that the party gets what they think they are getting. These types of analyses can be a win-win for both parties. I will provide reports showing future cash flow and net worth so each party will understand and can plan for their near term and future financial needs.

Divorce has many financial pitfalls that can be avoided by getting the financial guidance of a CDFA. Not all assets are created equal. A $50,000 IRA is not equal to a $50,000 stock account. The tradeoff of home equity with an equal dollar amount of other assets may look equal at first glance but after applying taxes, capital gains, cost of sale, etc., they can actually be very unequal assets.

The marital home has the most financial pitfalls associated with it. Especially for women, there is a lot of emotional connection and perceived stability with the home. She doesn't want to uproot the kids and cause more emotional distress. But a home, while it is supposed to be an appreciating asset, is illiquid and can end up being a money drain. I meet a lot of divorced women who regret keeping the home. The marital home is a big reason why divorced women end up with a low standard of living. I want to help people understand their choices and not make financial decisions in a vacuum which often happens when there is not a financial expert involved in the divorce.

How I help couples decide on a settlement?

Knowing the long term implications of a proposed settlement is critical to understanding the effect on both parties and their financial wellbeing and that is where the value of a CDFA comes in. This seems straightforward to me, and yet most divorce settlements are not decided in this manner. Where a financial expert is not involved, divisions are often being decided based on a snapshot picture of a financial situation, and not on a long term analysis. Misinformation and misconceptions about how one or both of the parties will live after the divorce is detrimental to the divorce process and can unnecessarily drive up expenses or lead to inequities. **If one party will suffer unequally in the long term as a result of a settlement,** *then the division was not equitable*.

After I have analyzed all of the financial information, I'll create settlement proposals as starting points. It is important to know that I am not an attorney and I do not give legal advice. My job is to show the long term financial effects of a settlement proposal. That is why my analysis includes reports showing long term cash flow and net worth for each party. Graphs and pie charts make visualization and understanding easier. These reports and graphs can be used by the attorney during negotiations or in court to support my client's case. If I am working with the couple together, then these reports and graphs can be used during the settlement meetings where I will facilitate negotiations using my mediation skills and help the couple find a solution that works for the family. Working together in this way can form a basis for the future interactions a couple with children will inevitably have.

Once a settlement is agreed upon, I draw up a detailed memorandum of understanding.

When couples hire me to help them through the settlement process, I recommend they employ attorneys to write the legal documents and I can guide them towards attorneys who will do that affordably. When a couple uses my services to settle their divorce, it is so much more affordable than using attorneys for the back and forth process of coming to a settlement. Even when you include the cost of hiring an attorney to prepare and review the legal paperwork, couples can often finish their divorce for much less than what <u>one</u> attorney will commonly ask for as a retainer. My process is also faster so they can go on with their lives.

What you can do before your divorce to reduce the stress of the divorce process

One of the worst positions you can be in when you are in the divorce process is having no access to the financial documents and being in the dark about your income and investments. I see this all the time, particularly when only one spouse handles the financial aspects of the marriage. My advice if you are thinking about divorce (and you probably aren't reading this book unless you are) is don't delay in getting your financial information in order! I won't go into detail here and list what you need to gather (you can find that on the blog on my website), but don't waste any time.

What happens if you are the spouse who doesn't have access to financial documents? Your attorney will bill lots and lots of time requesting documents from your spouse's attorney. Deadlines will be missed and/or information will drip, drip, drip out. Some documents may be withheld altogether to hide assets. Is this against the rules? Yes. Does it happen? Yes.

Meanwhile, you have no idea what your financial situation is. You may also be in the unfortunate position of not having access to money, so the process of getting financial information bleeds you dry of every financial (and emotional) resource. Often the other spouse stops support payments, knowing he or she has you over a barrel financially. You may have no choice but to settle, often in the dark about the true financial picture. Unfortunately, in these situations I lose some of my ability to help. Both attorneys and I need financial information to help you.

Even if you are involved in the finances, and have them at hand, you could be caught in a situation where your spouse moves out and takes the financial documents or you move out and leave them behind. This can happen unexpectedly-the straw breaks the camel's back, and within days someone moves out. Maybe you come home to find your spouse, your belongings and the financial files are all gone.

Ideally documents should be saved as PDFs on your computer and saved on a flash drive which you leave with a trusted friend or family member or at work. Hopefully you can quietly gather documents but you may need to ask for the records. There is no need to go further than explaining that you have a desire to learn about your finances and be involved. If your spouse doesn't provide documents before you split up, can you imagine what it will be like after you split up? Besides, it truly isn't a bad idea to scan your important financial information and keep that offsite. Your house could burn down!

After you have gathered the financial information, hopefully you are on your way to financially educating yourself on the family finances. If you are going to divorce, you will need to learn what your expenses are (believe me many people really have no clue), how to budget and how to manage bills. Now is a good time to start learning.

Other things you need to do to prepare for divorce that will make the process less stressful are:

- Plan where and how you will live

- Figure out how your children will be cared for if you have to return to work

- Get your car fixed or replace it (during the divorce is not a good time to have your car go kaput)

- Brush up on your job skills or go back to school, if needed.

- Read about how children will react to divorce, so you can be a better parent and help them through the process.

Children react to divorce in similar ways based on their age

- Seek counseling.

- Establish an emotional support group. You will need it!

Other forms of divorce

I've been in a legal or financial profession almost all my life and sometimes I forget that the average layperson knows little about the legal system and does not understand the process of divorce. Below I'll explain the other methods of divorcing and a summary of how each one works.

Pro Se or Do it Yourself Divorce

Pro se divorce is where one or both parties represent themselves and do not have an attorney. In North Carolina, forms are available online from the NC Bar Association and this is the case in many other states as well. Many state bar associations provide legal aid for those who cannot afford the services of an attorney. But there are pitfalls associated with this. First, with no legal or financial advice, parties make errors. For instance, in North Carolina, claims for equitable division (claiming part of the assets) and alimony <u>must</u> be claimed before the divorce is final. If you fail to do this in advance, then you can't do it later. For a very simple divorce, where there are no children and little assets, a pro-se divorce might work out OK.

Mediation

Mediators are third party neutrals, usually attorneys, trained in alternative dispute resolution techniques, to help divorcing couples identify and resolve issues. In North Carolina and in many other states, mediation is required before certain issues can be brought to trial in family court, such as custody or equitable division trials. Because of these rules, most cases end up in mediation, but not before both parties have paid out a lot in legal fees.

Similar to going to a CDFA, couples can go to a mediator and settle their divorce. But there are differences. Mediators are not supposed to give advice and they almost never give financial advice. While neither I nor a mediator can give legal advice, as a settlement facilitator, I give financial guidance and will point out the financial effect of proposed settlements.

At mediation where both parties have attorneys, the parties are paying the mediator and they are each paying their attorney. Each side is in a separate room, and the mediator shuttles back and forth, trying to come up with a solution. Attorneys are doing what they are hired to do; advocate for the most for their client. I can't help but compare this shuttling back and forth to the telephone game you played as a child, where words and meaning are lost or misunderstood along the way.

I'm glad mediation exists so at *some* point, the parties have the opportunity to try to settle. Where a couple cannot work together towards a settlement, mediation is the next best solution. In some cases, such as more acrimonious cases or where child custody is being negotiated, I will team up with a mediator. Whether I work with a couple by myself or with a mediator, when I work with parties to facilitate a settlement, we meet and collaborate together, so each party understands the others viewpoint and the financial result of any proposed settlement.

Collaborative divorce

Collaborative divorce is a progressive method of divorce that has caught on in some areas of the country. Each party has their own attorney and other professionals such as child therapists and financial professionals (like CDFAs) are involved. The parties meet together which makes it similar to my settlement process. However, when three or four professionals are in a room, this method can get quite expensive.

The unique aspect of collaborative divorce is the Participation Agreement ("PA"). The PA is a written agreement which says that each party must exchange complete financial information and maintain absolute confidentiality (meaning they cannot use the information or discussions against their spouse later if they don't settle). The PA also requires that, if after holding settlement meetings an agreement is not reached, the professionals must withdraw from the case.

The positive aspect of collaborative divorce for clients ready and willing to settle is that the attorneys involved have no financial incentive to drag the case out. However, for this same reason, many attorneys are not sold on the idea of collaborative divorce. Though there are many settlement minded attorneys out there who I have the pleasure of working with, there are those who want to bill as much as they think their client is able to pay and they purposely drag out the process.

You should be aware that for this reason, many attorneys will talk about collaborative divorce but never enter into a PA, taking away their incentive to help you settle. If you think collaborative divorce is an option for you, make sure a PA is signed when you hire your attorney.

Hiring attorneys (and what you need to know):

You've probably gathered by now that I don't care for the attorney driven divorce solution that is so predominate in the U.S. However, I realize that some people have no choice but to hire an attorney. There can be legitimate reasons why one spouse or both need the power of the court and the expertise of good legal counsel.

Even for those who agree that a financial expert like me is the right solution for a *financial settlement*, I recommend to my clients that they understand their legal rights before negotiations. This can be achieved in a number of ways. Many state bar associations have attorneys available that can provide free or low cost consultations. If you are a member of a flat monthly free legal service, such as Legal Shield, you can access legal advice that way. If you are savvy enough, you can google and read the statutes that apply in your state. Many attorneys give free consultations. Beware of attorneys who tell you that you should "fight for your rights". That is code for "you will pay a lot of legal fees".

Having worked in the legal field for the first 20 years of my professional life, I understand how the legal profession works. Here is what you need to know:

It bears repeating that attorneys are professionals trained to advise and protect people's legal rights, and they must have a depth of knowledge in all areas of the law in which they practice in order to represent their clients adequately. It is not fair or reasonable to expect that they will also have the depth of knowledge that a CDFA has about taxes, pension distributions, insurance issues, long-term ramifications of property division or financial planning.

1. An attorney is barred from representing parties. That means if you want attorneys to handle the division of your assets and debts, child custody and support, and post-separation spousal support and alimony, two attorneys must be hired. That's expensive. In my area, a common family law attorney retainer is $5,000. Multiply that by two and that's $10,000 just to start.

2. Attorneys charge retainers because they want to be assured of payment for their services. There is nothing

wrong with that. I ask for one too. As they bill, the retainer is used and once it is fully used, they will usually ask for another deposit. If they don't use it, they *should* refund the difference. Be aware that some attorneys keep any unused retainer (they just call it something else). That's a big problem if you decide to reconcile, settle early or want to fire your attorney. I was recently told by a woman that she hired an attorney who shortly thereafter moved to another firm. The old firm would not refund her retainer and the attorney asked this unfortunate person for another retainer. She could not afford it and ended up divorcing pro-se. Talk about stress!!! My advice if you hire an attorney is to read the fine print about retainers and clarify when you will get a refund of your unused retainer.

3. Attorneys bill by 10 or 15 minute increments. That means if you speak to your attorney for three minutes, he or she may bill the minimum 10 or 15 minute increment. Do not use your attorney as a therapist! If you need information and not advice, call the secretary first, the paralegal second. Be aware that paralegals bill in those same minimum increments, just at a lower rate. There is a lot of pressure, particularly with young associates, to bill. Their financial contribution to the firm has a direct relationship to their salary and their partnership track.

4. When a client hires an attorney to settle a divorce matter, it becomes a litigated dispute. The attorney is there to further their client's rights. The intent is to prove why the other side's position is wrong and your side is right. The attorney makes the decisions, and the client follows along. There is a progression through pleadings, discovery, motions, negotiation and then trial, if necessary. Many attorneys are reluctant to deviate and move to negotiations before pleadings and discovery has been completed. This in itself makes the process costly.

5. Unscrupulous attorneys will not negotiate until they think you are running out of money. Because attorneys make the decisions, if one attorney, but not the other, would like to begin settlement negotiations, negotiations will not occur. Most attorneys approach the negotiation process by writing letters back and forth. Don't you think it would be less costly and more productive if you could sit in one room and negotiate each point and resolve your divorce in hours?

6. It's said that less than 5% of divorce cases go to trial. Many times when a trial is scheduled, settlements are reached before the parties go to court but after they have paid their attorney for the long and expensive process of

preparing for trial. The predominant form of resolving divorces is negotiation and settlement.

Why hiring a CDFA and settling your divorce is The Right Divorce Solution

Getting financial advice in a divorce is critical. Imagine knowing that you will be OK in retirement. Even in cases where there isn't enough money to support both households, wouldn't it be better to know that you will have to make adjustments rather than be faced with an unpleasant reality years later?

I can't squeeze blood out of a turnip, but I can use my knowledge of tax laws to save money and my skills at financial planning to make the best out of your financial situation, and then educate you on where you stand. There is always loss on both sides in divorce. To think otherwise is not realistic. If you had to pay more or receive less from the settlement than you were anticipating, wouldn't you feel less resentful if you knew you were not being treated inequitably?

Then there is the emotional side. Dragging out a divorce is hugely stressful. It affects your health, ages you, and adds financial stress that might continue on for years. The sad thing is, people start down the road of "fighting for their rights" and the battle to win becomes its own entity. The law is not fair, and the only winners are the attorneys. By settling, you can get on with your life and find happiness.

Let go of winning, and try compromising. Think about whether you will really benefit from taking sides. Are you really that far apart? Are you realistic in your expectations and are you getting advice that is in *your* interests? How much better off will your children be when you put their interests first? Wouldn't you feel better knowing what your financial future holds? Wouldn't you like to get on with your life, put this in your past and discover your next life chapter? Why not have a kinder, less fearful, more affordable and financially smart divorce by hiring a CDFA? It's The Right Divorce Solution.

Call me for a free half hour consultation

I believe it is important for people to contact me early in their separation process. I provide a free half hour consultation. Many couples are still amicable at this time and would like to divorce amicably. During this free consultation I discuss how my solution works and how I might be able to work with them in their particular situation.

I have worked with clients in a variety of ways and most of my clients are women. My preferred method of working is with both parties as a financial neutral. People have also hired me because they want to know where they may end up financially if they decide to divorce. Sometimes hiring an attorney is unavoidable or someone learns about my services after they hired an attorney and they realize that they need help on the financial side. In that case I act as their financial advocate and provide analysis and reports to help support their case. I also provide specialized services such as QDRO facilitation, pension valuations and present value calculations for buyouts.

I regularly post blogs on my website, providing information to help people divorce in a better way.

Helping my clients goes beyond being a CDFA. An important side benefit is that I guide my clients towards other competent professionals such as mortgage brokers, bankers, realtors, estate planning attorneys, budgeting professionals, health insurance agents and financial advisors that can help them get their house in order after the divorce.

Mary Salisbury is the founder of The Right Divorce Solution, LLC, and is located in Wilmington, North Carolina. She can be reached at (910) 622-7180 or by email at Mary@TheRightDivorceSolution.com. Her website is www.TheRightDivorceSolution.com

MIKE TOBUREN

Founder & Attorney at Law

Toburen Law, PLC.

Email: mike@toburenlaw.com

Website: www.ToburenLaw.com

LinkedIn: www.linkedin.com/in/miketoburen

Twitter: https://twitter.com/toburenlaw

Call: (616) 425-9212

Attorney Mike Toburen provides comprehensive legal services to the West Michigan community. Mike is genuinely committed to his clients. Mike takes an adviser's approach to law to ensure not only that his clients are well represented, but that they also thoroughly understand each step of the legal process.

As an established attorney in the greater Grand Rapids area, Mike specializes in family law, estate planning, and business law. Mike is known in West Michigan courts for his aggressive representation and his compassionate nature.

Mike Toburen is committed to West Michigan. Born and raised in Hastings, Mike attended Hope College in Holland as an undergraduate, began his professional career in Kalamazoo, and attended law school in Grand Rapids.

A proud member of the local community, Mike is an active volunteer and serves several area organizations including the YMCA, Mel Trotter Ministries, Legal Aid of Western Michigan, and the Andrew Elliott Rusticus Foundation.

COMMON MISTAKES DURING DIVORCE
By Mike Toburen

Who's your ideal client, Mike? Who do you help?

My ideal client is someone who is either already divorced and is having trouble with the now ex-spouse in terms of operating within the parameters of that divorce or someone who is facing a divorce who wants to protect themselves and their children.

An ideal client for me is someone who wants to protect themselves but also is willing to work towards an outcome that is fair to both sides.

What are some of the most common obstacles for people in, or going through divorce?

Without a doubt, the main obstacle is the stress and pain that is caused by divorce. Even if one of the parties wants a divorce, there usually is a lot of pain involved on both sides. One of the fears people have is that one party will win in a divorce and the other party will lose.

It's very easy, especially early in the process when it's new, the pain is still very real as both parties realize that the marriage is going to be over. It can be very, very difficult sometimes for people to realize that there is a middle ground, especially in terms of custody and parenting time. There does not always have to be a win or lose proposition for either party.

The second obstacle when there are minor children is finding a custody and parenting time schedule that will allow both parents to have enough time with the children. In Michigan, the law says that children should have enough parenting time that they can have a strong bond, a strong relationship, with both parents.

That can really be a challenge, even if the parents end up living in the same community they were living in before the divorce, especially when you factor in jobs and the children's school and other activities. If one of the parents ends up moving some distance from where their home was when they were married, that obviously adds a whole other layer of challenges.

The third obstacle that I see is compiling an accurate summary of the party's assets and debt. This can be especially true for middle to upper class clients, where there are significant assets, which can include multiple investment accounts, rental properties, and the corresponding debt. It can just be a lot of work to get an accurate picture. If you were going to say we're going to divide all of the assets 50-50, as simple as that might sound, determining the total value can often be a challenge.

It's also a challenge or even maybe more of a challenge if one of the parties was primarily responsible for managing the finances, and the other party wasn't quite as involved. At that point there are two ways to go about putting together an accurate list of assets. One is to get the cooperation of the other party, which can be done informally if that party is willing. The other option to do that is through the discovery process.

How have you helped somebody to overcome one, or a combination of those obstacles you just mentioned?

I had a client and in this particular case I represented the wife. I would classify this couple as upper middle class. She was a mother of two young children, and she was a stay at home mom and was not heavily involved in managing the couple's finances during the marriage. Her husband decided to leave her and he filed for divorce.

In this case, there were two immediate challenges: One was that my client did not necessarily want to be divorced. Part of my job was being a counselor on the personal side, helping her understand that as much as she didn't want this to happen, it was going to happen. She had to find a way to engage in the process to make sure that she was protected and that we could reach a result that was fair to her.

We had to use the formal discovery process, which meant that we sent out interrogatories, which are a list of questions that are mailed to the opposing party that have to be answered under oath. Although the answers to our question will be written, the answers are considered to be under oath. It's similar to a deposition, the difference being that it's done through writings instead of verbally.

It was also a challenge in this case to put together a complete list of the parties' assets. The benefit to my client was making sure we had an accurate list of assets. In most cases, both parties will voluntarily disclose any assets and debt, because they know that they're ultimately going to have to do so. In this case, the other party, the husband, and his attorney, were not willing to do so. Which is why we had to use formal discovery.

It added more time and cost to the process, but the estate and the marital assets were substantial enough that the end result made it worth my client's time and money to do so.

Share 2-3 of the most common misconceptions for divorcing couples going through a divorce?

The biggest misconception I see is thinking that the court, a judge, has to make every decision in the divorce. Instead, the court would prefer that the parties resolve as many of the issues as possible, to avoid the costs of litigation, but also to free up time for the court to handle other issues.

In Michigan, there are steps built into the divorce process to encourage the parties to resolve issues. One of them is mediation, where the parties meet with a neutral third party in hopes of finding middle ground on issues like parenting time, child support, and property division.

I have clients that will ask me - If we agree to a parenting time schedule that is unusual, maybe one parent will have very little parenting time during the school year and will have more in the summer - Will the court allow me to do so? In most cases, the answer is yes because the court wants people to resolve their own issues.

Misconception number two is that each issue is a win or lose proposition. In reality, it's very rare for either party to get everything they want. I will have clients tell me that the other parent has this issue or the other parent really doesn't spend quality time with the children, so he or she should not have any parenting time or should have very little parenting time. There are cases where that is appropriate, but in general the court wants both parents to have ample parenting time with the children, because children do better, children are healthier, when they have a strong relationship with both parents.

On issues like child support or property division, the starting point is that marital assets will be divided 50/50. The same goes for marital debt. That can change a little bit either way, but it's very rare for one parent to get most or all of the marital property and the other to get none.

The third misconception in terms of custody and parenting time is the perception that the court will favor mom over dad in a custody dispute. That may have been true years ago when it was much more common for mothers to be stay at home moms and handle most of the child raising responsibility.

I'm comfortable saying now that most judges are fairly neutral in regards to custody and parenting time. Obviously, for a baby who is nursing, mom is probably going to get more of the overnight parenting time. As a general statement, most family judges are neutral, again in regards to the question of should we favor mom or dad based on gender.

What are some of the biggest pitfalls divorcing couples may not be aware of?

Number one is not following a court order during the divorce process. In the state of Michigan, from the day the complaint is filed, if there are minor children, the divorce cannot be finalized for six months. During that time, there can be temporary orders that are used to manage parenting time, child support, access to the home, etc. Not following one of those orders usually is very detrimental to that party.

A lot of the issues in a divorce are he said/she said. Not following a court order is very cut and dried - an order is either followed or it is not. A party that does not follow a court order usually suffers the consequences.

Pitfall number two is that once parties begin to separate their finances but before the divorce is finalized, it is a very common and very detrimental mistake for one party to begin to spend money lavishly. Until the divorce is finalized, even if the parties shut down the joint checking account and open up their own separate accounts, that money is still marital property. If one party buys a new vehicle, he or she may end up having to compensate the other party for half the value of that vehicle, because that other party still has a right to half the marital estate.

I always tell clients in a divorce, be very, very careful spending money on items that are not necessary. Pay the bills, take care of your children, and wait until the divorce is final to spend lavishly on yourself.

Mistake number three, when there are minor children involved, is allowing a new boyfriend or girlfriend access to the children. Most judges prefer during the divorce process that parents do not allow their children to meet and spend time with a new significant other. If a judge has to make a custody and/or parenting time determination, it usually works against the parent who has introduced a new boyfriend/girlfriend to the children.

Psychological studies show overwhelmingly that it is detrimental to children to meet mom's or dad's new significant other, either during the divorce or even right after the divorce is finalized.

It's hard enough for children to see their parents separate and divorce. It's even worse when there are new significant others brought into that relationship. The children need time to adjust to one change, which is mom and dad no longer living together. They don't need to adjust to a new change, which is a new significant other. I have seen judges do one of two things in this situation - either issue an order that for some amount of time, it might be just until the divorce is finalized, it might be six months or one year after the divorce is finalized, but an order that the children cannot be around the new signification other.

I've also seen judges issue orders that are a bit more extreme, and take away a parent's parenting time if they have already introduced the children to a new signification other. I tell clients who are dating during the divorce, spend time with them when the other parent has parenting time with the children. When you have your children, be focused on your children. I even advise that for six months after the divorce is final, that they are very, very careful about introducing their children to a new signification other.

What are 2-3 of the most common fears you hear from divorcing couples?

One fear I see a lot from clients is the fear that if I compromise on one particular issue that I have shown weakness that will make it more difficult for me to hold firm on another issue. I see this very, very often where a client will say, "I'm willing to accept less than half the marital assets. I can provide for myself, or I think it's fair," for whatever reason, "I'm afraid to give in on that portion of the divorce because I don't want to give in when it comes to parenting time."

Part of my job is to help my clients realize that a judge or a court will never hold it against a client that they compromised on an issue. In negotiating with the other party and/or the other party's attorney, clients will sometimes see it as a sign of weakness that they compromised on an issue, and that the other party or the other attorney will take advantage of it.

I have to educate and help my clients become comfortable that it's better strategy to be willing to compromise on an issue that is less important and if they're really going to dig in their heels and fight for what they want on another issue, that actually works to their advantage.

The second common fear is helping clients face the reality that life is going to change. It's going to change forever, even for the party that filed the complaint for divorce. It's a very stressful time. Parents are aware that their children are going to suffer. It can be very stressful on finances, where you had two parents working together to pay the mortgage and buy food and all of the day to day expenses. Now you have two households to manage. It might be a mortgage and it might be rent. It can be a very, very stressful time.

Sometimes early in a divorce, if one party really, really is hurt or really doesn't want the divorce, part of my job is helping them engage in the process, helping them start to set some goals and start to envision and see for themselves what the new reality will look like. Again, there's definitely a personal component in addition to the legal component.

The third fear is that clients are naturally afraid that they're going to lose. Part of my job is to help my client realize that it's uncommon for one client to lose and one client to win. I tell clients often that when the divorce is over and the judgment has been entered, it's more than likely that both parties are going to feel like they got a portion of what they wanted, but not everything they wanted.

It sounds obvious, but why would someone want to get divorced in the first place?

There are two common patterns when it comes to divorce. One is that both parties realize that the marriage just isn't working. It happens where both parties realize that it's just a very negative, sometimes a hostile situation, and it's very unhealthy for the children.

The other pattern is that one party decides that he or she is done with the marriage, regardless of how the other party feels. If one party to a marriage wants a divorce, the other party cannot stop it.

Why is that better for the parties?

If the parties have children, they have to find a way to co-exist after the divorce is final. They have to find a way to work together because they have minor children and those children are going to be co-parented for some amount of time. If issues can be resolved during the divorce as opposed to litigating those issues, the parties can start the healing process before the divorce is final. Ideally, you want both parties to a divorce to begin searching for compromise, begin searching for solutions, especially when there are minor children involved.

When parties fight over every single issue and their divorce only ends after a trial, it is then very difficult post-divorce for the parties to immediately begin to work together regarding parenting time and other issues involving the minor children. Something as simple as attending a child's sporting event at the same soccer field or in the same gymnasium can become acrimonious and stressful.

Again, the sooner the parties can work to resolve some of their issues, the more likely they are post-divorce to enter into a new relationship where they can co-exist and do what's best for the children.

What led you to this field?

People will often ask me why I focus my practice on family law. It seems to be an area of practice where people are in very stressful situations. My interest in family law began during law school. At the outset of law school, I had no intention of focusing on family law. I interned for a family law judge in Kent County, Michigan during law school, and I realized at some point during that semester that I would focus on family law when I began to practice law.

For me, I saw an opportunity to truly help people. Family law is a lot more than helping people get divorced. It's helping people during a very difficult time in their life and helping people build a new life post-divorce. Helping my clients come up with a parenting time schedule or helping my clients move forward with their finances post-divorce is very rewarding.

I help my clients protect themselves and their families. I do that by representing people during a difficult time, and helping them reach an outcome that will not only be good for them, but will be good for the other party and most importantly will make sure that their children are provided for post-divorce.

What's the most import thing people should think about when they are looking at their options for divorce?

I would advise anyone who is hiring a family law attorney to make sure they hire someone they can trust. That might seem like an obvious answer, but I don't know that people always spend the time to meet in person and interview an attorney before they hire that attorney. I always advise a potential new client that we should meet in person before they hire me. I get a feel for what their goals are. They get a feel for how I do business.

As an example, if a client comes in and says, "I'm going to file for divorce, and I'm going to take everything. I don't want my soon to be ex-spouse to ever see the children." If I feel like that potential client is being vindictive or just wants to be hurtful, that's probably not a client that I want to represent, and I would probably recommend that that person hire someone else.

On the flip side, I want my clients to trust me. I make commitments to my clients. They hear back from me no later than the following business day if they leave me a voicemail or send me an email. I tell potential clients before they hire me that I will fight for them, I will represent them to the best of my ability, but I will be professional and respectful to the other party, opposing counsel, and the judge.

What's the best way for divorcing couples to learn more about how you can help with their divorce?

I offer a free 30 minute initial consultation. I think we should get to know each other a little bit, make sure that we can trust each other, and make sure that I'm comfortable with the goals that the potential client is trying to achieve.

My phone number is (616) 425-9212.

I can also be reached by email at mike@toburenlaw.com and on my website, which is www.toburenlaw.com.

Clients can also email me directly through my website. I also have close to 100 blog posts that provide a lot of good information regarding family law and other legal issues that people face. Potential clients and clients can educate themselves on some of the family law issues that they may face during a divorce.

LISA ANNE BYRNE, CDFA

Certified Divorce Financial Analyst

Second Saturday Twin Cities

Email: Lisa.anne.byrne@gmail.com

Website: www.secondsaturdaytwincities.com

LinkedIn: www.linkedin.com/in/lisa-byrne-ba16b9137

Facebook: SecondSaturdayTwinCities

Call: (612) 518-6000

Lisa Byrne, CDFA (Certified Divorce Financial Analyst) has been working in the financial services field for over 20 years. Lisa specializes in working with clients pre divorce and helps them prepare cash flow analysis, budgets and financial statements. During the divorce process Lisa works closely with clients and their attorneys in analyzing spousal support proposals, asset splits, social security maximization, and other important financial issues.

A CONVERSATION
with Lisa Anne Byrne

Describe the kinds of people you serve and the various types of situations they find themselves in when they come to you for your help.

The clients I serve are people who are contemplating divorce; in the beginning stages of the process or those that are stuck and having difficulty moving forward. What I have learned over the last several years is that people contemplate divorce for several months or years. The sooner I can work with someone; the better understanding they will have of the process and will be able to make better decisions for themselves and their family.

The majority of people I serve are women and they tend to be in the age group of 45-65. In general, the people who seek my help have been married 20+ years; have been contemplating divorce a very long time; are not the most familiar with their family finances; are seeking guidance and want to understand the process. 70% of all divorces are initiated by women and women are more likely to reach out and ask for help; so I conduct monthly workshops on Divorce. We explore the Financial, Legal and Emotional/Social aspects of divorce.

I use three words to describe my process – Control, Confidence and Closure as a way to guide people through the process. The people who attend my workshops are looking for control over their lives, financials and futures. They want to know where do they start. What steps do they need to take to move forward, and put some control around a situation that is not only extremely difficult emotionally, but financially and legally difficult as well?

What common obstacles prevent the people who you work with from managing their Finances when getting divorced?

In divorce, I see education (particularly financial education) as the number one obstacle. Statistics show that one in five women fall into Poverty after divorce. It is important to understand the many reasons why this occurs. In a two income family you have two partners sharing expenses; childrearing and meeting financial obligations. We know that women, still on average, earn about 78% of what a man earns; women have more time out of the job market to take care of extended family members and children; and women are the primary caregivers when their children are young. Oftentimes this means they have not been in the workplace as long or have achieved the same promotions and salary advancement as their partners. The homemaker may not have kept up the necessary credentials for career advancement and oftentimes needs several months or years to get their careers back on track.

And of course women live longer which puts an additional financial burden on someone who is single. Even if you work until you are 70, most people today will live well into their late 80's and 90's and that is a long time to live on your savings.

Share an example of how you've helped to overcome those challenges and what kind of transformational results you were able to gain for them.

A fairly common example of a challenge is when one spouse believes their partner has an addiction. Gambling and alcohol are the most common problems. When the addiction is Gambling; I encourage them to seek immediate legal help and begin the process fairly quickly. It doesn't necessarily mean that they have to quickly divorce but you need immediate help in protecting your assets. I strongly suggest the person view their credit report, adds additional security measures on their accounts and protect assets with legal measures as quickly as possible. When the addiction is gambling; quick measures are necessary.

Another example of a transformational result was a woman who attended our workshops and was being pressured to quickly sign a settlement proposal. I strongly suggest that you never sign an agreement when you are under pressure. Take time to review the proposal, and seek legal advice before signing. This particular agreement was very one sided and unfair to her. We (the professionals who present at our workshops) were able to review it with her; help her hire an attorney and the final settlement was significantly more beneficial to her than the original proposal.

What are some of the most common myths or misconceptions your clients have about divorce?

I would say the biggest myth and misconception is that all divorces are litigated. Very few divorces are actually litigated; and most are settled. There are many ways to reach settlement agreement mediation, cooperative and collaborative divorce and variations of all three. The other myth is that somebody wins and somebody loses. First thing I tell a client when they meet with me is that this going to be painful. This is not a win or lose. This is about compromise. If they're willing to work with their spouse, if they're willing to come to a settlement and agreement; both sides should feel a little bit of pain.

Nobody wins in a divorce. You're closing out a chapter in your life or oftentimes a long book. I remind people that at one point they loved this person and cared very deeply for this person. Marriage begins with a vision and a plan for the future and when it ends it is very painful. Divorce is not a win or lose situation – it is a compromise and a dissolution of a business agreement.

Another myth is that the court or attorneys care about fault. In the majority of states divorce is no fault. Whatever the issue (unless of course there are criminal activities such as abuse) the court, mediator or attorneys don't really care whose fault it is. The divorce process is about is a fair and equitable settlement for both parties.

What are some of the pitfalls that divorcing couples need to be aware of when managing their finances throughout the divorce procedure?

I would say the number one pitfall is the availability of liquid assets. Unfortunately divorce is a cash hungry business. Your attorney is going to need a retainer; you may need to move out of your home and rent a new place. You may need to pay for additional childcare; new household furnishings or maybe even another car. Liquid assets (not retirement accounts) or the availability of credit is very important.

Another major pitfall is not being prepared. The first thing that you need to do in a divorce is to prepare a budget and cash flow. You will save yourself a great deal of money if you are prepared. Start to think about your budget and how you will manage your finances when you are separated and divorced.

And you are going to need records and details of your finances. You will need statements from your retirement accounts, checking, savings, and your credit cards. Are your accounts joint and opened since you were married? Did you have accounts before you were married? Did you make a down payment on your house with premarital assets? Don't overlook records and don't underestimate the values on your home or personal property.

Your tax bill is not an accurate assessment of the value of your home. Most likely you will need an appraisal to capture the current value of your home. And it is important to understand tax consequences. A dollar in a retirement account is NOT equal to a dollar in the equity in your house. A retirement account is pretax dollars that you'll pay taxes on it when you retire or if you need to take some money out for cash needs.

Another pitfall is mixing money and emotion. The email you write at midnight when you are tired, angry and lonely will cost hundreds of dollars by the time it is answered and reviewed by all parties involved. **Don't mix money and emotion!**

And another important pitfall is not getting good advice. Assemble a team of professionals you trust and want to work with through the process. Interview them, ask for referrals and make sure it is someone that will work in your best interests. Understand whether the professional you hire is working as a neutral or an advocate – an important distinction.

Always hire an attorney that specializes in family law; you don't want someone that does this part-time and is not familiar with local customs, judges and officials. Most states have regulations around child support but spousal support is more nuanced and can be very different by judge and counties. It's very important that your family law attorney have a relationship with the family court system in the county you in which you will be filing.

What are some of the most common fears about getting divorced?

The main fear for everyone getting a divorce is the fear of the unknown. When you married you dreamed of a new life and began to make plans for the future. You built a home; started a family, and suddenly all of that changes when the divorce is finalized. Fear....What will I do? How will I do it alone? What do I need to do next?

It is important for me to give my clients a sense of control. Here's where you start.... step one. My job is to help them devise a plan of action; educate them on the process and give guidance on how to execute to execute their plan. I see the difference in their faces when they have a "To Do List". My clients tell me, "Now I can begin to see my future because I understand the process and know what I need to do next. It is going to be different but I will be ok." My goal is to help my clients overcome their fear, and help them move forward.

Fear of the future is paralyzing for people going through divorce. One of the most important aspects of my job is to give guidance and vision to their future. What does it mean financially to be divorced? The attorneys provide the legal closure and the therapists help clients in dealing with the social aspect of divorce. Divorce brings a great deal of change into someone's life – and that is our 4th C. Where you live might change. Your friends will change. Control, confidence and closure and Change.

It sounds obvious, but why would someone want to get divorced in the first place?

People come to me contemplating divorce for many different reasons. Some have a specific issue that needs to be addressed such an addiction like gambling or alcohol. It is not uncommon to see someone who have been dealing with an alcoholic spouse for many, many years. And of course there are instances of abuse both emotional and physical.

Outside of specific issues, oftentimes it's, "We've been married for 25 years; the children are gone and we have nothing in common. Our lives are very different than they were when we go married. I want the next 25 years of my life to be different". It is very sad but I am seeing that this is a common thread among baby boomer women. When they reach 55 and 60 and they realize they have not been happy for many years. They are the ones that most embrace change and are actively seeking it. Women very seldom prioritize themselves; it is children, family and friends first. They begin to envision their life very differently and realize they would like to separate from their partners and move forward. It doesn't always make sense to me but I never judge; that is not my job. My job is to educate people on the divorce process and do it in a way that you doesn't leave a path of destruction behind them.

I remind clients is that if they are a parent, they will be one for the rest of their life. That means you will attend graduations, weddings and funerals. You'll see your ex-spouse on many occasions and if you can divorce in a way that does not leave you both mortally wounded you will not regret it. All divorces are different but if you can forge a path that's open to communication; you will be a good example for your children and extended family.

Your outcome for a better future is more easily achieved if you can do it in a way that is constructive as opposed to destructive.

Could you tell us a little bit about your background, education, and your experience as it relates to the topic of divorce and managing finances in divorce?

I began my career in finance as a mortgage officer in Chicago. Mortgages are very transactional and I was interested in helping clients with long term financial decision-making. I decided to get my MBA in finance and administration in the early 2000's. I began my career in financial services just as the financial crisis hit in 2007... perfect timing!

As difficult as those times were for people what it taught me was the importance of devising a financial plan and not be driven by emotion when it comes to investing. I devoted a great deal of time in learning about the family law area and began to specialize in working with women going through financial transitions such as divorce or loss of a spouse.

My credentials are the CDFA, which is a Certified Divorce Financial Analyst and CRPC, Chartered Retirement Plan Counselor.

I currently do 2 – 3 workshops per month for people going through the divorce process. I teach the financial aspect and bring in professionals from the legal and counseling fields to help with the program.

The workshop is part of a national program that's called Second Saturday. It was first introduced 25 plus years ago in California by two women financial advisors. My program is called Second Saturday Twin Cities and I do the workshops in a suburban location the second Saturday of every month in a three format and a shortened version in downtown Minneapolis on the second Tuesday of every month. I work with an amazing group of professionals; a mediator parenting consultant; family law attorney, and marriage and family therapists.

My goal for the workshops is to become a resource guide for people that are contemplating divorce. Instead of sitting down at a computer and searching family law attorneys and other professionals I offer vetted resources that are available to the people who attend these workshops. The people, when they leave our workshops, have a much better vision of what the need to do next and how to proceed.

My part of the process is predivorce work and financial planning. For people going through divorce a settlement focuses mostly on the current situation and it rarely focuses on the future. Because my clients are predominantly women, I know how important is for them to have a clear vision for their financial future. Women statistically live five - to ten years longer than men. For divorced women our planning needs are very different than they are for men. 64% of eligible men remarry within 2 years and the numbers are much lower for women. When you take into consideration that women have earned less in their lifetime, and women stay single and live longer, we're at a disadvantage.

A realistic budget and projections are crucial for achieving a comfortable retirement. Where are you going to live? Who is going to take care of you as you age? My entire business really is not only about what a client is doing today, but it's what their future is going to look like. I help my clients achieve their goals by listening to them very carefully –assess their current needs; how they view money and what defines their view of success and philanthropy.

What would be your best tip for someone looking at their options for divorce?

The best tip would be to take control of the process. Understand that you can only control what you do and you cannot control what others do or how they will respond to a situation. Don't leave a path of destruction behind you...look forward and envision your own future. Be a role model for your family, your friends, and particularly for your children. If you do then your children can look back on you and say, "I have no doubts that my mother and my father both love me. They were just not meant to be together for the rest of their lives".

Hire a therapist to work through your own issues so you don't repeat mistakes. Make sure you are making the right decision...divorce is final and if you aren't sure, spend time working on your marriage and try to make it work. If you make the decision to move forward with a divorce, surround yourself with a great group of professionals that will guide you through the process.

If the reader wants to know more, how can they connect with you?

You can find me on my website: www.secondsaturdaytwincities.com.

On Facebook: Second Saturday Divorce Workshop. LinkedIn: Lisa Byrne – Owner of Second Saturday Twin Cities. You may also email me: Lisa.anne.byrne@gmail.com, or call: (612) 518-6000

MARCO CLAYTON BROWN, J.D.

Divorce Attorney

Founder of Brown Law, LLC

Email: marco@utdivorceattorney.com

Website: www.utdivorceattorney.com

LinkedIn: www.linkedin.com/in/marcocbrown

Facebook: www.facebook.com/utdivorceattorney

Call: (801) 685-9999

I was born in Oregon, and grew up in a little Alaskan village. Like eighty-five people little. My dad ran a salmon hatchery and my mom was an air traffic controller. I spent a lot of time hunting, fishing, and playing with my dogs.

I started Brown Law in 2010 on the floor of our fourth-story condo. At the beginning, there were no clients and no network. Since then, we have been blessed to help thousands of Utah families through divorce.

When I'm not working, I'm with my family. My beautiful wife, Demaree, has a doctorate in opera performance. Our son is a ham who loves bowling and often refers to himself in the third-person.

I read. A lot. It's usually about history, law, or business. I don't read much fiction, but when I do it's probably Steinbeck or Kafka.

I cook too — Italian mostly. My favorite food is pizza. (Not Domino's or Papa John's; the real stuff you find on spaccanapoli in Naples.) Pizza is how we know God loves us.

And to keep weight off from all that reading and cooking, I hike or lift weights.

MONEY & DIVORCE
By Marco Clayton Brown

Let's take a moment and have an honest discussion about money and divorce.

How Money Problems Lead To Divorce

To start, money fights is one of the most common reasons for divorce in America. It might be that a couple doesn't have enough money to pay bills, so they fight. (Being poor is super stressful.) It might be that one spouse committed financial infidelity and hid credit card spending for years. And it might be that one person tries to save money, but the other simply won't stop spending every penny.

Whatever the underlying money problems might be, the effects are the same: stress, fights, and, if not corrected, divorce.

So, is it a given that if you have money problems you'll get divorced? No, but the likelihood goes way up. You can't expect to play with fire and not get burned.

The Situation Most Of Our Clients Find Themselves In When They Come To Us For Help

Since we're divorce attorneys, we tend to see people at the most difficult time of their lives. Their marriages are ending and their families are breaking apart. They're scared. They worry about not having enough money, and about losing friends.

As you can imagine from what I've said so far, we often serve people who don't have enough money because there's almost never enough to go around in divorce.

The reason for this is because (1) people with money problems tend to divorce, and (2) you use more resources when you get divorced because you give up economies of scale and specialization.

More resources means more money, and since there wasn't enough money to begin with, there certainly isn't enough during divorce. You see, most people live right up against their financial precipice, so there's no slack in their money system. One thing goes wrong — and divorce definitely meets the criteria — and they're over the edge financially.

In fact, many of our clients don't know the basics about their financial situations. They usually have a general sense things aren't going well, but they don't know specifics.

For example, they don't know the full extent of their debts. I can't tell you how many times I've heard someone respond to the prompt "Tell me about your debt," with the following: "I'm not sure. I know we have credit card debt, but I don't know how much. Maybe $10,000 or something like that. Then there are the cars, but I'm not sure how much we owe on those. And the house, I think we owe maybe $200,000 on it. I just don't know. My husband took care of the finances." Many people don't even know what they make per month at their jobs, much less what their spouse makes at his or her job. They've never had to think about the answer, I guess, because they make ends meet by using credit cards.

When People Come To You For Help, What Plan Do You Give Them For Getting Their Financial House In Order?

When people come to us, they don't know what to do. They're lives are falling apart and they need a plan. We provide our clients with three different plans. First is a legal plan to help them accomplish their goals in divorce (e.g., obtain primary physical custody of the children). Second is a plan to help them and their families deal with divorce on an emotional level. Third is a plan to help them get their financial houses in order.

What I'm about to share with you is our seven-step plan for helping our clients get their financial houses in order.

Step #1: Determine Your Yearly Family Income

I'm amazed at the amount of people who don't know what their household income is.

To get a handle on your money, you need to start by laying out every source of income that comes in to your family every month and every year.

For an average family, this process is straightforward. You look up your pay stubs and see what your yearly salary is, and then you do the same for your spouse's pay.

Sometimes, though, a family may receive income from many different sources, like: rental properties, trust fund disbursements, investment dividends, stock options, royalties, child support payments, alimony from a prior marriage, etc.

Whatever your family's situation, and whatever your incomes sources, lay them all out so you know exactly what the source is and exactly what the amounts are.

This is the foundation for your financial house.

Step #2: Inventory Your Assets and Debts

Immediately after figuring out your income situation, sit down and do a deep dive into your assets and debts.

Before I go on, I want to define what I mean by "asset" and "debt." An asset is anything you own free and clear. A debt is anything you make a payment on. So, if you own a home, but you are making payments on the mortgage, then that home is a debt. It only becomes an asset *after* you've paid it off in full.

With those definitions in mind, start by inventorying every asset you have. Make a spreadsheet and write it all down. Do your best to assign values to each asset. For example, if one of your assets is a car, find the value on Kelley Blue Book. Total everything up at the end so you can compare it to your total debts.

(Note: when it comes to personal property items like clothes, jewelry, kitchen appliances, it's okay to use categories and estimate values. It takes too much time to value every single item.)

After inventorying your assets, do the same thing for your debts. I'm talking every credit card, every car payment, every mortgage, everything you owe money on. Get current balances so you know what your debts are right now.

When you've pieced together all your debts, subtract them from your total assets. This figure will give you your total net worth — keep in mind that you might have a negative net worth. To be honest, your total net worth, while interesting, is not nearly as important as having put together an item-by-item asset and debt list.

There is real power in knowing exactly what you have and exactly what you owe.

Step #3: Determine Your Average Monthly Expenditures when You Separated from Your Spouse

One very important number you will use again and again during divorce is your average monthly household expenditures at the time of separation. (Separation is usually the date you and your spouse stopped living under the same roof.)
You'll use this number to calculate alimony, as well as asset and debt allocations. It can also sometimes be used as evidence regarding child support obligations. It is, perhaps, the most important single number in a divorce case.

To do this correctly, you will need to figure out what you normally spent per month on food, mortgage, gas, utilities, and everything else. It's no easy task and it can take a long time, but, like I said before, this is an incredibly important number you'll use throughout your divorce.

So, take your time and get it right.

Step #4: Put Together a Bare-Bones Budget

This budget is completely different from the step #3 budget. The step #3 budget is a representation of your standard of living during the marriage. This budget is all about figuring out the lowest amount you can live on if you had to.

The reason I have our clients put together this budget is because there's almost never enough money to go around during divorce. Our clients have to face the real possibility there won't be enough money to go around, even if you receive child support and alimony.

In the end, if you know what you can survive on, it helps relieve stress and create a realistic financial plan for your family's future.

(Hint: I use everydollar.com to put together our family budget. It's incredibly easy to use and takes only minutes per month. Just keep in mind that to build an accurate bare-bones budget, you need to account for every single dollar coming in *and* going out. This will take time in the beginning, but you'll get the gist of it within a couple months, and then it'll become second nature.)

Budgeting Success Story

As part of our commitment to helping our clients succeed with money during and after divorce, we offer a free budgeting and finance 101 class. Clients can come as often as they would like, and we encourage them to attend as much as they need to catch the vision.

I remember one lady — let's call her Lois because I've been watching *Superman* lately — who came in for a Roadmap and Recovery Session. Lois ended up not hiring us, instead she hired an attorney she went to high school with, but wanted to attend the budgeting and finance 101 class we offer.

Lois needed some help with budgeting because she, like many, let her spouse handle the finances. She had never put together a monthly budget before because she never had to. Now, everything had changed and she had to take control of her finances, otherwise it wouldn't be pretty.

During Lois's class, we discussed family budgeting and how to pay off debt. She took to the training like a fish to water. I explained the system my family and I use to budget, which cut our family spending by at least 25%. We talked envelopes and cash storage systems. We really got lost in the weeds; it was great.

After the class, Lois went home and implemented the system. She's had good success with it ever since. In fact, Lois still emails me every few weeks to ask questions about the system and how to run it more effectively.

Lois is succeeding with money during divorce, which means she'll be successful after divorce. And it all started with her monthly budget.

Step #5: Create an emergency fund

As you go through this journey of getting your financial house in order during and after divorce, you'll need an emergency fund.

An emergency fund is nothing more than some money you set aside for, you guessed it, emergencies. Stuff happens. Bad stuff happens. And when it does, you need some cushion to pay for it.

In our experience, if you don't have an emergency fund, you tend to get sidetracked and off the plan. And when you get off the plan, inertia tells you to stay off the plan. That ain't good.

Start with an emergency fund of $1000 if you can. It's that just too much, start with $500 and move up to $1000. The point is to put money aside so you can stay on the plan.

Step #6: Pay Off Your Debt

This step might seem ridiculous in the context of going through a divorce. I mean, how is anyone supposed to pay off their debt during divorce?

Look, I'm not going to lie, paying off debt in the best of times is tough (or we tell ourselves it is), and it's super tough during divorce. That said, I've seen lots of people pay off their divorce debts.

The nice thing about our system is we set the stage for paying off debt in steps 2 and 4. When you know your debts, and you have a bare-bones budget follow, you will almost certainly have slack in your system that you can use to start paying off debt.

But which debt should you pay off first?

I suggest, as does Dave Ramsey in his fantastic book *The Total Money Makeover*, that you list your debts smallest to largest (smallest principal due to largest principal due), and then you pay the smallest debt first, working your way up to your largest debt.

(Hint: one thing I've seen many people going through divorce do to jumpstart their debt payments is use their share of the equity from the sale of the marital home to pay off credit cards and the like. I think this is an incredibly good idea since getting out of debt after divorce is so much better than buying a new home and burying yourself and your family in new debt.)

So, why is it important to pay off debt?

First, it's important because paying off debt is almost always the quickest way to build wealth. When you don't have interest payments, you can invest your money and start accumulating wealth. If you have personal debt, however, that debt weighs you down and takes away from your ability to create wealth.

Second, it decreases stress. Debt creates stress. I know because I had a fair amount of debt after law school, including my wife's masters and doctorate degrees. It weighed on me every day. I lost sleep because of it and carried tension in my jaw because of it. The day we paid off our debt, I felt that stress leave my body and mind. It was wonderful. That's what paying off debt will do for you.

Third, marital debt represents an anchor weighing you down. In a very real way, getting rid of marital debt represents you moving on from your divorce and leaving it in your past. You'll be free to create a new life without debt or your divorce holding you back.

Step #7: Invest

Once you've paid off your debt, it's time to start investing heavily and creating serious wealth for you and your family.

Now, I'm not an investment guru, and I don't pretend to be one, so I'm not going to tell you which stocks to pick to hit it big. Instead, what I will do is give some basic guidelines that have been helpful to me personally and our clients generally.

First: invest something every month.

Investing needs to become a habit, and the only way to create a habit is by doing something over and over and over again. Even if you can only invest $25 per month, do it. What you'll find is that $25 will turn into $50, which will turn into $100, and so on. Get started. Create that investing inertia. That inertia will grow over time.

Second: automate your investing.

Here's the easiest way to automate your investments: have money automatically removed from your paycheck and put in your investment account. You can easily do this with your company's 401(k) for example. The reason automation is so powerful is you never see the money in your account, so you don't miss it.

Third: Keep it simple.

People think that investing is some incredibly complicated endeavor. This fear of the complicated paralyzes people into not taking action, so they end up parking their money in savings, which is about the worst thing you can do. Investing doesn't have to be complicated. You can find very good, straightforward investing strategies in a lot of places.

For example, investing in index funds is a simple solution that helps keep investment costs down. An index fund is a type of mutual fund that tries to mirror a part of the stock market. For example, an S&P 500 index fund would try to mirror the S&P 500, so your investment returns would be about the same as the total S&P 500. These funds generally have very low costs, which is good because costs tend to eat up your investment returns over time.

Another option for keeping things simple is to use what's called a robo-advisor. You can think of a robo-advisor is an online investment advisor who primarily uses computer algorithms to make investment decisions. Wealthfront and Betterment are the biggest robo-advisors. They're incredibly easy to use, and they individualize your investments depending on how much risk you want to take. They also automate your entire investing process, which makes it more likely you'll invest month in and month out. Additionally, a robo-advisor's fees are low compared to traditional investment advisor fees.

Fourth: investing is a marathon, not a sprint.

"Get rich quick" is a euphemism for, "Lose all your money fast."

If you want to grow serious wealth for you and your family, you have to think of the investing process as a marathon. Of course, a marathon lasts only a few hours — well, if you're like me it might last a few days; running is the worst of human activities — but investing lasts a few decades. It's all about discipline and vision.

Create a simple investment plan. Automate the system. Stick with that system until you and your family have created serious wealth.

That's how you do it.

That's It; That's our Seven-Step Plan to Get Your Financial House in Order

When clients come to us for help navigating divorce, these seven steps are the plan we give them for getting their financial house in order.

Again, implementing this plan takes effort and thought. I can tell you, though, if you follow these steps, you'll find yourself head and shoulders above almost everyone else. You'll change your family forever and build serious wealth for you and your children.

The Major, Unforeseen Pitfall our Clients Face when Implementing our Seven-Step Plan

Any path to success will have its twists and turns. Putting your financial house in order during divorce is no different.

The major, unforeseen pitfall we've seen when people implement our plan is that no matter how good your budget, no matter how well you plan and map things out, emergencies happen. Cars break down, kids go the ER, whatever.

Now, this sort of thing isn't completely unforeseen, right? We have an emergency fund for this very reason. Still, you'll be surprised how often stuff happens and how often you may need to dip into your emergency fund as you get your financial house in order.

Again, the purpose of the emergency fund is to build cushion in to your financial system. If you don't have that cushion, you're way more likely to get off track with your budget and not get back on the plan.

So, emergency fund. Start with $1000 if at all possible. That's a pretty high number for someone getting divorced, I know, so maybe start with $500, then move up to $1000.

What Is the Role of Credit in Getting Your Financial House in Order During Divorce?

I have been asked more than once what the role of credit should be in getting your financial house in order during divorce.

When clients ask this question, they're really asking, "How much debt should I go in during divorce?"

As you can imagine, I'm not a fan of credit because credit is just a way of saying debt. I don't like debt at all. I think debt allows people to live beyond their means, make poor decisions, and then pay for them for years. It increases stress levels and has contributed to more marital breakups that I can count. It's bad news.

With that in mind, I think the priority of anyone going through a divorce should be (1) to not use debt if possible, and (2) to get out of debt as quickly as possible.

Regarding credit scores, I don't really worry about them. I want people to focus on never using credit. I want them to pay off credit cards, lines of credit, mortgages, and all of these other debts that have caused them so much pain and stress over the years.

Focus on getting unshackled from debt, not on improving a score that will allow you to get more shackled. Only then can you build real wealth for you and your family.

What's the Best Way to Pay for a Divorce Attorney?

With all this talk about paying off debt and getting your financial house in order during divorce, one almost inevitable question comes up: how should someone pay for a divorce attorney?

Divorce attorneys are expensive. Sure, you may find a cheap one, but is that really how you want to go? Do you find the cheapest knee surgeon for your replacement surgery, or do you find the best because it's important to have the best? Same principle applies with divorce attorneys. Find the best attorney you're comfortable with and spend the money necessary to secure your future and your family's future.

And, back to the question: How do you pay for that attorney?

If there's any way to pay cash for the attorney (i.e., not go into debt), do that. Here are a few examples of how our clients have paid their bills without incurring debt.

Lean on family for support. Talk to everyone you can and see if they will help you. It'll be uncomfortable, yes, but if it's your best option, do it. Moms and dads are the most likely to help.

Sell a car or some other high-ticket item(s). It's important to keep in mind that (at least in Utah), money spent on a divorce attorney is marital money, so there's really nothing wrong with selling some marital property to pay for a divorce attorney.

Use savings or cash out some investments. Nothing wrong with this. It's better than incurring debt. I will caution you, however, about taking out a loan on your 401(k). That's an option for many, and the loan usually has a low interest rate, but it's still debt. If you can cash out assets instead of incurring a low-interest loan, cash out the assets.

Save up. If I've learned one thing since becoming a divorce attorney, it's that most people think about divorce for a long time before actually getting divorced. This means you may have time to plan and save. Figure out what the average cost for a divorce is in your area, and save up that money. When you do, you'll know you won't need to go into debt to get through divorce.

And what if those options just don't work and you can't get the money together to pay cash for a quality divorce attorney?

Sometimes, you just don't have the means to pay cash. I meet with lots of people who, because of domestic violence or drug abuse, have to get divorced *now*. They don't have time to save, and no family member will give them the money.

In situations like this, you have a choice. Either you go with a cheap attorney (or no attorney, depending on your situation), or you incur debt to pay for a high-quality divorce attorney. The first option leaves you and your family exposed and largely unprotected. The second provides peace of mind that you'll be taken care of.

As much as I don't like debt, if you find yourself in a "get divorced *now*" situation, I would counsel you to hire an attorney and ensure you and your family are protected.

I have met very few people who regretted spending money on a high-quality divorce attorney. I have met hundreds who regret not hiring an attorney or hiring a cheap attorney.

When they have to incur debt to pay for an attorney, most people use credit cards. I would suggest finding a lower-cost alternative if possible. A personal loan at a credit union might carry a lower interest rate. A 401(k) loan is an option. Loans from family are great as well, if you can get one. Do whatever you can to minimize your debt load.

My One, Best Piece of Advice

I'm going to wrap up soon, but I wanted to leave you with my one, best piece of advice to help you get your financial house in order.

Here it is: create a monthly budget. And I mean a real budget that accounts for every dollar coming in and going out.

This may sound simplistic, but If you create a monthly budget, you will figure out what all of your debts and assets are. You'll figure out where you spend too much and where you can save. You can use those savings to pay off your debt, and then start investing to create wealth for you and your family.

It all starts with a good monthly budget.

Thank You

Thank you so much for taking the time to read this chapter. I hope it has added value to your life, and I hope it will help you get your financial house in order.

If you would like more information about divorce, we would love to give you our Divorce FAQ's book. It answers the most commonly asked questions about Utah divorce. All you have to do is call **(801) 685-9999**, tell us you read about the offer in this book, and request a **free** copy. We'll email it to you that day.

Also, if you are in the Salt Lake City area and would like to attend our **free** budgeting and finance 101 class, we'd love to have you. Again, all you have to do is call **(801) 685-9999** and sign up.

RICHARD M. GORDON B.A., M.A., J.D.

Principal Mediator at
A Fair Way Mediation Center

Email: rich@afairway.com

Website: http://www.afairway.com

LinkedIn: www.linkedin.com/in/rich-gordon

Facebook: www.facebook.com/AFairWayMediate

Call: (619) 702-9174

The principal mediator at A Fair Way Mediation Center, Rich Gordon has helped hundreds of people throughout San Diego and beyond to settle their differences through mediation. A graduate of the University Of Kansas School Of Law, he also holds an M.S. from Rutgers. He trained as a mediator at the University of Connecticut.

HELPING COUPLES BREAK UP NICELY

By Richard Gordon, B.S., M.A., J.D.

Open the door to my office most any day and you'll find couples from all walks of life. Some will be older, working through issues surrounding the unraveling of a long-term marriage. Others may be a successful millennial couple who are dividing assets acquired during their domestic partnership. And, because we are based in San Diego, you will find Military Couples who coming to us for a mediator well-versed in Military benefits and constraints. Also, our doors are open to same-sex couples, either married or in a committed partnership who have selected us to help disentangle their family and financial obligations. And sometimes you might come across me sitting in front of the monitor balancing a relationship teeter-tauter via a long-distance mediation process on Skype or FaceTime.

Whatever the demographic, our mission is to help "couples break up nicely."

Many years ago, while in a "country lawyer" style practice on the East Coast, my role was as an advocate attorney. I fought hard for my clients. Not all were involved in family matters, but plenty of times I saw the damage done by animosity and pettiness and how it impacted children's lives, parental relationships with their kids and even general family of origin dynamics.

At the same time, it became clear that battling for position, struggling for victory day in and day out, was taking its toll on me. Professionally and personally. It was clearly time for a change. Mediation seemed logical; methodical; kind and gentle. There are no winners or losers. The outcome is fair to all. That's why we named our firm A Fair Way Mediation Center. Our logo features two people looking at each other eye to eye.

Divorce mediation services can help with any issues that should come up in the break-up of a marriage, including child custody and visitation; child and spousal support; post-high school education costs, life insurance benefits, pension and social security questions and many more topics.

After extensive mediation training at the University of Connecticut I learned anyone who is willing to make a good faith effort to mediate their dispute can and should mediate. So long as each party is willing to explore various options and not be closed minded to the concept of compromise, mediation can work well for most participants. Even if the communication between the Parties is very difficult or non-existent, mediation may still be appropriate. Mediators know it is crucial to have open dialogue with each party. We use certain ground rules in order to create a safe environment so our clients can work through difficult issues and reach Fair, Reasonable and Equitable Marital Settlement Agreements.

Simply put, divorce does not have to be the legal and emotional "war" that society tends to make it out to be. It is entirely possible to have a civil and even amicable marriage dissolution through such recourses as mediation. However, for that to work out, both parties must take certain steps to reach a mutual agreement; otherwise the mediation process can fall apart due to one or the other spouse's refusal to be open to the process.

A divorce mediator acts as a neutral third party and does not tell any either spouse what to do. Instead, the mediator's job is to level the playing field, keep the communication going, brainstorm possibilities, offer options, and guide the divorcing couple to mutually agree on outstanding issues. We avoid the concept of "Winners" or "Losers" and instead create a contract which is fair to both parties as well as to the children of the marriage.

This chapter will help ensure the success of your mediation sessions, while exploring who benefits from mediation, the financial and emotional aspects of mediation and the advantages of pre-nuptial mediation.

Preparing for mediation

Here are several dynamics to take into consideration when you prepare for mediation and divorce:

Do you and your spouse have a solid level of trust? Since mediation is a voluntary process, parties are not legally forced to reveal various documentation, and they must trust that the other person will disclose all the essentials. If one spouse is unwilling to disclose items such as asset lists, debts, or other financial information, then it can hinder reaching an agreement. This does require a certain level of maturity and emotional control on the part of either party—one of the main goals any mediator will aim to establish.

It may seem simplistic but when considering mediation, remember it cannot be done with only one spouse actively involved. Both partners must also agree to pursue mediation. Point in fact, at A Fair Way we insist that whoever initiates the first call has their spouse call as well. Each party must feel comfortable with the mediator before they ever walk into our front door. This ensures the equanimity of the sessions and keeps the playing field level, with the mediator squarely unbiased. A mediator does not take sides. It's our job to be the fulcrum of a teeter-tauter and to keep the process as fair and balanced as possible.

Furthermore, recognize that the mediator is not there to determine who is right or wrong in a divorce settlement. Their sole purpose is to remain as a neutral party, helping spouses work through any unfortunate negative emotions while protecting both parties' rights and interests. You shouldn't fear the mediator taking your spouse's "side" during sessions, but also know they will strive to give your partner just as much a fair hearing (and results) as they give you.

If your spouse is resistant to the idea of divorce mediation or clings to several misguided beliefs about the mediation process, they may well sabotage proceedings or refuse to attend altogether. Helping them understand the great benefits of mediators in divorce, however, can often turn around a stubborn spouse's opinion on the matter. This is why we always encourage phone calls from each party before we actually meet.

Along with both parties being ready to commit to the mediation process, there MUST be FULL DISCLOSURE of all the assets and debts accumulated during the Community Property period of the marriage or domestic partnership.

Failure to disclose may be considered fraud by the Judge with the withholding party being forced to surrender all the asset and not just 50%.

A prime example of this fraudulent situation is the case of a California woman who did not list a Twenty-Five Million ($25,000,000.00) Dollar lottery winning ticket on her disclosure form. Instead she kept the ticket hidden from her husband during the negotiation phase. Once the judgment of divorce was granted she turned the ticket in for the prize. The event was covered by local news. The now ex-husband took her back to court asking for half of the winnings. The judge said, "Sorry sir, you do not get half, you get it ALL because your ex-wife committed fraud."

This is just one glaring example of the importance of being honest and open within the mediation sessions.

Ensuring Success

The most important way you can prepare for mediation is to ask yourself if you are ready for divorce.

Marriage can have its ups and downs. With divorce rates about 40% (higher for second marriages, and even higher for third marriages), it's easy to understand why so many couples consider divorce when their relationship is on the rocks. Infidelity, financial problems, children, abuse, and substance or gambling addiction are some of the most commons reasons why people divorce, as they feel betrayed, hurt, or unloved. Even if you're not at the point of separation yet, we can help navigate the choppy waters of disagreements over property, or keepsakes like grandma's good china and silver. Some couples seek out mediation in preparation for divorce even if they are not yet ready to pull the trigger to end their marriage. They want to know what the end produce may well look like. Often when a couple sits down and looks rationally at the costs of breaking up, they may decide that it could be (as the saying goes)" cheaper to keep her."

When considering divorce, at least one spouse (and sometimes both) is not ready to end the relationship. Here are a few questions to ask yourself before making this life-altering decision:

1. *What are your needs and is your spouse meeting them? Do you know if your spouse is capable of meeting those needs?* Before you file for divorce, commit to joint-meetings with a therapist for several sessions and openly discuss your situation with your mental health professional. You may want to enter therapy on your own so you may focus on

your personal feelings and needs first, then. When you're ready to have an honest discussion and mutually work on your relationship together you and your partner can undertake therapy sessions together. If you have very specific problems you want to work on, a family mediator may be able to help also. Marriage is a two-way relationship and it must work for both partners. If therapy or mediation works, it was worth it. If it doesn't, it is still valuable, as you can tell yourself you've tried your best to make the relationship work, and you won't have any regrets down the road.

2. *Are you staying in your marriage because everyone around you tells you this is the right thing to do? Or are you considering divorce because others tell you that you'll be better off?* Remember, this is your life and therefore your choice, so take your time. You'll be the one facing the consequences so you want to be sure you're ready to accept your fate.

3. *Are you really ready to face life and all of its financial responsibilities on your own? Can you become financially independent if you get a divorce?* Before filing for divorce, make sure all your papers are in order and your financial path is clear. Don't count on Spousal Support as your sole source of income. If you have not worked for many years

it's time to get retrained in a field which interests you and will provide an adequate standard of living.

4. *Can you handle life's disappointments and ups and downs on your own? Do you have a strong support system of family and friends you can rely on when you need emotional or physical help?* Planning is everything and you want that support in place before you need it. It may be time to eliminate the nay-sayers from your life and instead surround yourself with positive reinforcement.

5. *If you have children, are you staying in this marriage for their sake alone?* If so, ask yourself if you'd want them to be in a marriage that looks like yours. If you can't find the strength within yourself to leave, do not look to your children for support and motivation. They should not be brought into the decision. After you've made your choice they can learn that walking away from a bad situation takes courage, especially when facing uncertainty. Prepare yourself for lots of questions. Life is going to look very different for everybody going through the divorce. Even the family dog will undergo change as one or more of the pet's best friends move away.

A few circumstances require you to make a major change in your marriage and living arrangements immediately, such as domestic violence, child abuse, verbal abuse, substance abuse and other addictions. Don't let the cycle of abuse start or last any longer. Leave immediately and take the children with you. If you're not sure what to do, call the Domestic Violence Hotline at 800-799-7233 for free, or call 911. Once removed from the situation, start counseling sessions for you and your children to address the abusing situation and the bullying behavior right away. You may want to consider obtaining a restraining order to keep your spouse away from you and the children while this behavior continues.

Remember that fear is a perfectly acceptable feeling when considering divorce. You'll be afraid of making a mistake, wary of what the future holds and how you'll cope. It's important not to let fear control your behavior and attitude. Divorce is painful for everyone involved, so the more amicable and collaborative you can be during the process, the better off you, your partner and your children will be. And remember that with the help of a family law mediator, you'll be able to reach an agreement in a few weeks, rather than getting tangled up in court for months or even years.

To ensure that your mediation progresses smoothly there are a few stumbling blocks and obstacles to overcome to ensure success. One of the first assignments a mediator will give you is to do your "homework". The more data you can bring to your sessions, the more quickly mediation will progress. Your mediator will most likely ask you to provide: Pay stubs; tax returns; bank statements; Retirement statements; mortgage statements; credit card receipts; appraisals of real estate; Profit and Loss Statements for any family owned business; and automobile loan balances.

Once you have gathered up the fiscal background, you and your mediator will have an easier time sorting out the.

Reconciliation vs. Divorce

As you can imagine, as a mediator, I see all sorts of folks in numerous stages of the relationship process. One of my favorite couples was an older Italian couple who had perfected the art of "arguing with love." During one particularly volatile dispute they decided that divorce was the only option. After spending a couple of hours with them it was clear they really didn't want a divorce. I told them to get the heck out of my office and resume their passionate marriage. And so, they did.

At the other extreme was a couple who had been married for more than fifty years. The husband came to the office with the assistance of a walker. The wife arrived pulling an oxygen tank. When I asked them why they wanted a divorce after such a long marriage the wife simply said, "It's just not fun anymore." For this unfortunate couple reconciliation was just not in the cards.

Many folks look to mediation to actually bring them back to being together. By the time struggling couples decide to hire a divorce mediator, one or both spouses have decided that the marriage has deteriorated so much, it is beyond saving and therefore should end. Spouses often agree on using divorce mediation instead of expensive and lengthy litigation when they believe they can handle all the issues relating to divorce, such as separation of assets and debt, child custody and visitation arrangements, and spousal and child support, and find common ground with few arguments.

While a family mediator may offer marital mediation and reconciliation services to help couples find solutions to specific marital issues, it's essential to understand that divorce mediation *per se* is not the same as marriage counseling. When you hire a divorce mediator, you are requesting help to get divorced in the most harmonious and least painful way possible, not help to save your marriage. If reconciliation is your ultimate goal, then marriage counseling with a therapist, or reconciliation services with a trained and qualified divorce mediator are more appropriate choices.

It is important to realize that most couples who have reached the decision to divorce consider it a point of no return. However, the uncertainty of the future, especially if the family home must be sold, or if there is financial instability, can sometimes cause a lot of worry and anxiety, which can lead one or both spouses to question if the divorce is a such good idea. That is why some spouses may agree to go to divorce mediation when their partner requests it, believing deep inside that if they agree with the other spouse on every point, they will be able to re-establish communication, peace and trust, and may be able to bring the marriage back together. The mediator needs to make sure that the party who quickly agrees with the terms suggested by their spouse is not being taken advantage of in the process.

Divorce mediation can still do a lot for a couple's relationship post-divorce. First, by acting as a facilitator rather than a judge or a referee throughout the divorce process, the mediator ensures that the rights and interests on both spouses are protected. Also, by not taking sides, he/she helps the parties decide what's best for all concerned and focus on a peaceful and conflict-free life after divorce, rather than dwell on past disagreements and resentments. Finally, an experienced divorce mediator has gone through intense training so that he/she can provide separating spouses valuable advice to improve their communication style and their problem-solving skills. Creating a new, more efficient communication channel and encouraging the preservation of this healthy communication after divorce will help ex-spouses when the need comes to solve more problems down the road, in a prompt and civil manner, especially if children are involved.

More economical, but not free

Another common pitfall or misconception folks have about mediation is that it is free. Mediators are trained professionals who are compensated for their time and expertise. In divorce mediation, the upfront retainer is usually between $1,500 and $5,000 – depending on the complexity of the issues involved and the level of disagreement of the spouses. Rarely will final fees exceed $10,000. Fees are usually equally divided by the parties.

With litigated divorces, costs can go sky high. Each party usually pays their own attorney a retainer of at least $5,000, and fees go up quickly from there. The average litigated divorce in San Diego costs $25,000. It is not unheard of for fees to exceed $1,000,000.

Some ask, we don't have any issues, what about a do-it-yourself divorce? With do-it-yourself divorces, or a paralegal "typing" service, you may only spend a few hundred dollars. However, you will not receive full legal information and may end up in court later – fixing mistakes or addressing issues you did not anticipate – at a much greater cost.

If it was a short-term marriage with no children; no children; no property to divide and no request for support payments then a do-it-yourself divorce may just do the trick. But if there are children to parent or property to be divided do-it-yourself divorce is simply not the most prudent wise choice.

In divorce mediation, most of the cost is for mediation sessions with the parties and the mediator. Unlike contested divorces where the lawyers have extensive "discovery" of the other party's assets and liabilities or lengthy depositions where all manner of questions are answered under oath. The end-product of the Mediation process is the Marital Settlement Agreement (MSA). This lengthy contract contains the terms created in the mediation sessions. The parties are encouraged to provide suggested revisions to the draft of the contract prepared by the mediator. The contract can only be signed once both parties approve the language and terms.

In litigated divorces, the costs are often driven by one party-who can force deadlines for discovery and hearings on the other party. This drives the other party's costs upwards. In litigated divorces, much of what you pay for you never see, including: legal research, preparation of numerous documents, telephone calls between attorneys, driving to court, copying and organizing documents. While many family law attorneys try to keep their fees reasonable for these services, the client may still feel left out of most of the process for which he or she is paying. In mediation neither party will even need to step foot into a courtroom. All meetings are either held in our offices or by Skype or FaceTime. Thus, costs are significantly reduced for the betterment of all concerned.

Saving More Than Money

For most couples, a divorce can be the cause of many difficult and stressful times. As challenging as a marriage on the rocks can be, a divorce is even more traumatic, especially if spouses choose litigation. Fortunately, many couples now try divorce mediation first to discuss and settle all issues surrounding their breakup. Most often, couples will opt for mediation because they hear it's less expensive than litigation. While they are correct, they often don't realize that mediation saves them more than just money. It can also minimize the effects of the emotional roller coaster they're about to endure. Mediators are trained to work through the process efficiently and with equanimity, keeping down costs.

During a divorce, spouses can go through myriad feelings--feelings that usually started during the marriage, way before divorce was even considered. Feelings such as heartbreak; sorrow; anger; frustration; betrayal; failure or confusion. On top of these multiple mental machinations a divorce produces a lot of stress. Stress about the future and the unknown, stress about finances and losing the family home or other assets, and stress about the well-being of the children, or the family pets. Divorce mediation can help couples reduce that stress level because it specifically aims at reducing conflict and negative emotions while working on reaching a settlement fair and equitable to both parties. With both spouses being in the same room for mediation sessions all topics can be discussed openly and frankly with an eye on reaching a fair, reasonable and equitable resolution of the issues which need to be resolved.

Because mediation is by definition not adversarial, it allows a couple to focus on the important issues without feeling combative or defensive. By acting as a neutral third party, the divorce mediator gently guides couples through the separation and negotiation process, addressing one issue at a time. The mediator helps keep animosity away while guiding couples toward conflict resolution that is acceptable to both spouses. The goal of divorce mediation is to allow spouses more control over their divorce process and to come up with an agreement that will work best for each of them and their children.

Divorce mediation can reduce stress in other ways, including reducing the length of divorce proceedings. A litigated divorce may last many months, or even years, especially if court hearings and contentious depositions are required. A mediated divorce can last just a few sessions, reducing the length of time for conflict between parties to continue. The goal of mediation is "Getting to Yes." That is an agreement fair to both.

Of course, a shorter divorce procedure also reduces cost, which can consequently reduce financial stress for both spouses. In the end, the shorter the divorce process takes, the sooner spouses can go on with their separate lives and begin the healing process.

And don't forget there are other proven ways to reduce stress during these difficult times, such as physical exercise, enough sleep, meditation, enjoyable hobbies, and surrounding yourself with a network of caring, non-judgmental people who can provide emotional and mental support.

Military Divorces

Being in San Diego, with one of the country's largest military populations, we have learned about the extra pressures of military life. Long-term deployments away from family and friends take a toll on the spouse and children left at home. Neither party truly understands what the other is going through while one spouse is stationed far from home. Communication is difficult to achieve on a meaningful basis. Unfortunately, these burdens often weigh heavy on military couples and divorce ends up being the only solution.

Getting a divorce is not an easy process for anyone, but for a military couple it may be even more complicated. There are often formalities, procedures and divorce rules that only apply to military families and can be confusing. Not only does the military have their own procedures, but the California Family Courts have their own set of complicated laws. Our mediators help military couples navigate through both these systems in the most expeditious and stress-free way.

For instance, as an example, one of the military laws to be aware of when seeking a military divorce is the Uniformed Services Former Spousal Protection Act (USFSPA).

A couple came in to our office recently who had been married for only three years. They were counting on both continuing to receive the same military benefits they'd received for the past three years. They were not aware that under this act to be eligible to continue to receive benefits—full medical, commissary and exchange privileges—required them to be married for at least ten years with the service member being on active duty for twenty. So too, to receive Military Retirement Pay the same 10/20 rule applies. Our team helped the couple weigh all their options and successfully worked out a resolution that satisfied them both.

This is just one of the subtleties that makes a military divorce slightly different from a civilian divorce. In nonmilitary divorces pension and retirement benefits begin on day one of the marriage. There is no ten-year threshold.

Besides military retirement pensions, other military benefits need to be addressed during a military divorce. Within one year of the divorce date, the former spouse can ask the court to designate him/her as a Survivor Benefit Plan (SBP) beneficiary. If the former spouse remarries before age 55, the SBP coverage terminates, unless that spouse's marriage ends in divorce or death. In regard to health insurance coverage, a former spouse is eligible to receive medical coverage under TRICARE if the marriage and military service overlap for at least 20 years and the former spouse hasn't enrolled in an employee sponsored health plan. As for the children, as long as they remain legal dependents of the service member after the divorce, they will be able to retain full military benefits until they reach the age of 22 or they get married.

Members of the military are afforded Post-911 educational benefits. This program will pay college tuition and provide a monthly stipend to the recipient for a period of time. These benefits can be transferred by the service member to one or more of their children or to their spouse if that is more appropriate.

It is important for the divorcing couple to understand both the civil code and the military regulations that apply to their unique situation. That's why using a mediator who is experienced in military divorce cases can be very helpful. The mediator can assist the couple in getting familiarized with the various state, federal and military laws in an amicable way before going through the divorce procedure, saving time and energy in the process. The local JAG office is barred from providing legal assistance when a divorce is the least bit contentious.

Fortunately, we can employ technology so that ---even when on deployment-- each party can be informed and participate in the decision-making process. Even if we can't be in the same room, Skype, FaceTime and Conference Calls allows us to share in the mediation process together.

Long Distance Mediation

In today's mobile society, military couples are not the only ones who can benefit from Long Distance Mediation.

Divorce isn't solely emotional separation – it's often also physical separation. One partner moves for their career, or to be nearer their family, or to make a fresh start. Another challenge arises when couples aren't able or willing to meet face-to-face, it was once an impediment to effective mediation. Thanks to modern technology, however, this is no longer the case – today divorce mediation can be facilitated through telephone, email, Skype, or any other method of video conferencing.

Long-distance mediation can be as effective and powerful as face-to-face mediation. There are a few simple factors to making long-distance mediation work:

1. Maintaining Neutrality: There should never be any solo sessions; all mediation activities should involve both partners.

2. Clear Technology: The connection, whether over the phone or the Internet, must be crystal-clear and reliable.

3. A Fair Schedule: The key is to start with the dates that must be locked-out due to individual schedules, so no one is ever prevented from participating.

Same Sex Divorce

Another growing niche in Divorce Mediation is same-sex divorce. We've been working with members of the LGBTQ Community long before the Marriage Equality Act. One of my favorite episodes in the myriad divorce sagas in our office was the couple who was amazingly kind and supportive of each other even after twenty years of marriage and three children. I asked (as I often do) "What is the reason for the breakdown?" The man confessed he was gay! His wife looked over at him with a grin. "Me too!" Despite living in the same house for all those years neither knew the other's "secret." Once the disclosure had been made, the process was about our mantra of "breaking up nicely."

It's easy to imagine why a divorce can be a cause of such difficult and stressful times for most couples. When LGBTQ couples decide to part ways, whether it involves dissolving a domestic partnership or a legally recognized marriage, they need to make similar decisions to heterosexual couples such as property and debt division, child support and custody, pet custody, spousal support, the division of retirement benefits received during the marriage; financial and tax issues, or health and life insurance. As the government has granted same-sex marriage equal rights, it is important for these couples to seek legal guidance and protection that will stand the test of time.

Until the late 1990s, California family law did not address the issues faced by non-traditional couples and many partners felt vulnerable, their future left to the mercy of the court. Since then, laws have changed to encompass many lifestyle situations. Today laws are changing even faster regarding LGBT families, and they may still differ greatly from state to state, which can make conflict resolution even more complicated legally. There has been a rise in the number of attorneys and mediators specializing in LGBTQ relationships so they can specifically meet the needs of this community. That is why it is important for you to choose a mediator who is highly knowledgeable in LGBTQ legal separation, domestic partnership termination, and marriage dissolution, and who has a lot of experience helping couples in these situations.

We suggest taking advantage of a mediator's free first consultation to evaluate if he or she has the experience in addressing the diverse needs of today's ever-changing families with sensitivity and understanding. Do not hesitate to ask if the mediation staff is specifically trained in same-sex couples issues and is sensitive to the nuances in these relationships.

When it comes to choosing between a divorce mediator and a divorce attorney, it is important to remember that mediation has many advantages. In many cases, it will be less expensive, less hostile and overall faster. Divorce and separation mediation enables LGBTQ couples to stay in charge throughout the process and handle their unique issues personally. Same-sex couples can make important life decisions together that they will be able to live with, instead of relying on third-party decisions made by attorneys or Judges.

How Long Does the Mediation Process Take?

One question that frequently comes up in our free consultation is "How long is this going to take?

While divorce litigation through the court system can last several months to several years and cost thousands and thousands of dollars, divorce mediation is often considered a less expensive and faster approach to resolving the disagreements separating couples may have. However, the time you spend in mediation can vary from several weeks to a few months, based on the conditions below, which are evaluated during your first meeting with the mediator:

How much you agree and disagree on at the time of separation. The more you agree from the start, the faster a divorce mediator will be at helping you resolve outstanding issues.

How many assets and debts you need to divide (i.e. distribution of property). Obviously, the more property there is to divide and debt to settle, the longer the procedure will take. You'll also need to divide tax responsibilities, as well as 401K, retirement and pension plans. During this stage, it is very important for both spouses to be honest and reveal all financial information, especially if they have assets or outstanding loans in their name only. A mediator may recommend hiring a certified financial planner to help you negotiate the division retirement accounts.

How you want to handle child custody and visitation time. While dividing real estate property and bank accounts may go smoothly, creating a child-sharing plan may be more difficult to complete without any disagreement. An experienced mediator can help you discuss the pros and cons of common custody arrangements so parents can reach a consensus that is in the best interest of the children.

How to assess child support and spousal support. While attorneys and mediators refer to a state calculator to assess child support and spousal support, other financial aspects may have to be discussed, such as the sharing of extra-curricular activities or additional medical expenses. Spousal support can also be awarded as one lump sum during the asset division instead of being distributed as monthly payments. A mediator can discuss various available options with the divorcing couple and assist with the decision-making.

The more willing to negotiate and complete the divorce process spouses are, the faster mediation will go.

Pre-nuptial Agreements

When we aren't in the process of mediating a separation, we are often called upon to help with a pre-nuptial agreement. This is an extremely valuable tool. Through the process of pre-nuptial mediation, a couple can stave off disharmony of the future, ensure that each is protected for the marriage and that should a disagreement end in divorce, the property division, child custody and support issues will be clearly delineated...supporting our mission of providing kinder and gentler ways to dissolve a marriage.

We firmly believe in the process and advantages of divorce mediation which is an excellent alternative to the aggressive and often stressful route of the courts that avoids the cost, length, and labyrinthine procedures, replacing them with a straightforward process of good faith negotiation with the guidance of a professional mediator.

A Prenuptial Agreement must be reviewed independently by either a lawyer or mediator for each party. If not properly scrutinized the whole contract can be knocked out by a court and be null and void.

Primary benefits of mediation

If you are considering mediation, consider these powerful benefits while making your decision:

- Safe environment

- Encourages exploration of all options

- Speedy and workable settlements

- No winners or losers

- Relaxed atmosphere

- Resolves differences

- No court appearances

If you are interested in learning more about A Fair Way Mediation, or mediation in general, please visit www.afairway.com or email rich@afairway.com or call (619) 702-9174.

ABOUT THE AUTHOR

Mark Imperial is a Best Selling Author, Syndicated Business Columnist, Syndicated Radio Host, and internationally recognized Stage, Screen, and Radio Host of numerous business shows spotlighting leading experts, entrepreneurs, and business celebrities.

His passion is discovering noteworthy business owners, professionals, experts, and leaders who do great work, and sharing their stories and secrets to their success with the world on his syndicated radio program titled "Remarkable Radio".

Mark is also the media marketing strategist and voice for some of the world's most famous brands. You can hear his voice over the airwaves weekly on Chicago radio and worldwide on iHeart Radio.

Mark is a Karate black belt, teaches kickboxing, loves Thai food, House Music, and his favorite TV show is infomercials.

Learn more:

www.MarkImperial.com

www.ImperialAction.com

www.RemarkableRadioShow.com

www.ingramcontent.com/pod-product-compliance
Lightning Source LLC
Chambersburg PA
CBHW060009100426
42740CB00010B/1445